The NANTES-
CANAL

a guide
for
walkers and cyclists

by
Wendy Mewes

The Nantes-Brest Canal
a Red Dog Brittany guide
3rd edition
published by Red Dog Books
ISBN 978-0-9935815-0-2

First published in 2007
Second edition 2012

British Library Cataloguing-in-Publication Data
A catalogue record for this book is available from the British Library

Red Dog Books is based in Somerset and in Brittany.
Enquiries should be addressed to the editorial office at
Red Dog Books, Poullic, 29690 Berrien, France.

email: reddogbooks@orange.fr

www.reddogbooks.com

CONTENTS

ACKNOWLEDGEMENTS

Special thanks to Charly Bayou at Le Musée de la Batellerie in Redon for his help and interest, and for providing photographs from the canal archive

Thanks for the work of Kader Benferhat, which has inspired so much interest in the canal

Thanks to the many accommodation providers who enlivened research for this book

FOREWORD

by Wendy Mewes

After more than a decade of long and short walks beside the Nantes-Brest Canal in all parts of Brittany, I can only describe my relationship with this remarkable waterway as a kind of friendship. For it has a distinctive, if sometimes mercurial, personality and character of its own, delving back into political and social history for roots in pre-Revolutionary times and offering in the present day an unparalleled perspective on the natural beauty of the centre of this region. My walking, research and discussions with canal professionals, inhabitants and recreational users have resulted in this practical guide (here in a new edition for 2016) and a travelogue - Crossing Brittany - recounting the more psychological and emotional experience of a journey along the towpath over the space of a year. The canal is so often a source of stimulating encounters and instruction about this most diverse, complex and rewarding land.

Anyone travelling in Brittany for any length of time cannot fail to be aware of the Nantes-Brest canal, which crosses all four departments as well as the historically Breton territory now called Loire-Atlantique. In this sense the canal has a symbolic significance beyond its own interesting identity and changes of fortune over the last two hundred years: it remains a physical link between the old capital Nantes with the adjacent Marches of Brittany, long fought over by Bretons and Franks, and the rural heartlands to the west.

In practical terms, the canal also provides a link between cultural and heritage centres across the region. To walk or ride along its 365km length is to discover settlements from ancient towns of half-timbered buildings such as Malestroit and Josselin, to tiny farming hamlets, rural chapels with their sacred springs, and châteaux ranging from the medieval towers of Blain to the late 19th century *château rose* of Trévarez.

Canalised rivers, which constitute the vast majority of its length, with all their meanders and caprices, furnish quite a different prospect from narrow, straight stretches of artificial canal, although some of these, like the Grande Tranchée near Glomel, are moving testament to the extraordinary potential of human toil.

The breath-taking variety of changing landscapes and natural environment along the canal is equally memorable. Flat marshlands in the east give way to heights of granite and schist, and wooded slopes lining the lush river valleys of the Oust, Blavet and Aulne, great rivers as striking in their individual character as the Bretons themselves.

The social and economic history of the Nantes-Brest canal is a remarkable story of vision, achievement, hardship and disappointment. Today, leisure use has breathed new life into this 'sleeping giant', but let us hope that over-development and the fatal temptation to turn interpretation into entertainment at every opportunity does not spoil the essentially natural pleasures of an exceptional resource.

I hope this guidebook will encourage readers to get out on the towpath and explore this singular and atmospheric waterway in all its many guises.

WENDY MEWES

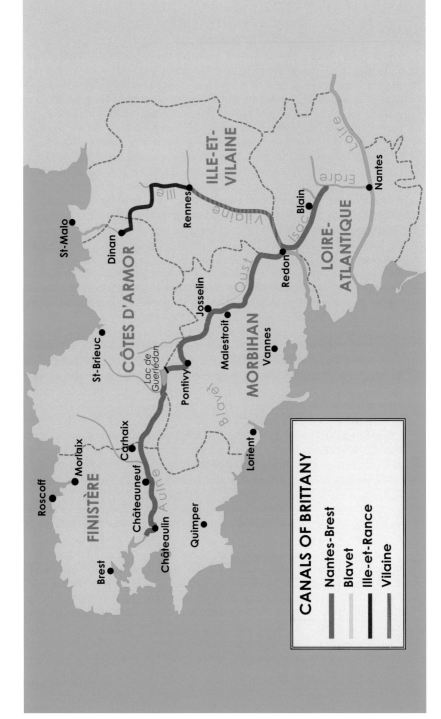

CANALS OF BRITTANY

Nantes-Brest
Blavet
Ille-et-Rance
Vilaine

ABOUT THIS BOOK

This guide to the Nantes-Brest canal is equally useful for walkers or cyclists planning long-distance routes and those who simply want to enjoy an undemanding stroll in pleasant surroundings.

The canal is a remarkable waterway, covering more than 360kms in its often tortuous route across Brittany, as the map inside the cover and on page 6 shows. Altogether, via canalised rivers and man-made channels, it flows through five departments, if a very brief appearance in Ille-et-Vilaine at Redon is included. Some idea of the differing flavours of the canal in Loire-Atlantique, Morbihan, Côtes d'Armor and Finistère is given on pages 30 to 33. On the map pages, the departments are colour-coded for easy reference of location.

The beginning and end of the journey from Nantes to Brest are along free-flowing rivers and not actually part of the canal. These do not have uninterrupted paths to follow their courses directly: many walkers begin at Lock 2 Quiheix and end at Lock 237 Guily Glas for this reason. For the more adventurous, a summary of the route from Nantes to the start of the canal proper, a distance of 21kms, is given on pages 34-37, and from the last lock at Guily Glas to the Rade de Brest (30kms) on pages 98-101.

A full introduction outlines the **history of the canal** from its original conception to construction, and heyday to decline, highlighting the enormity of the task and the remarkable achievement of the men who built it. Details of canal structures and the workings of locks are also included here. A full list of the 237 locks is given on pages 125-126.

The main section of the guide consists of a **detailed analysis of the canal and towpath route**. Each page, covering up to 10kms, includes a scale map, with locks, roads and settlements clearly marked, and distances to important places within easy reach of the canal. A distance in kilometres from Nantes is also shown on each map.

The map pages also carry **illustrations and details of attractive sights**, as well as facts about the canal and snippets of historical interest.

The guide is illustrated throughout with **colour photographs** of the canal and its constantly changing scenery at different times of year, as well as places of interest along the route and in the close vicinity

Colour-coded references to **accommodation** (brown), **refreshments** (green) and **provisions** (blue) are located on these maps and a large circular symbol on each page gives the connecting reference for fuller information/contacts for these establishments, which are listed on pages 112 - 123.

Travelling along the canal one cannot fail to notice the many coloured waymarks and signposts that refer to **walking circuits, long distance walking routes, cycle rides, *velo promenades* and VTT circuits**. The points where these walks and cycle rides <u>leave</u> the towpath are marked on the maps and a large square symbol gives the page reference to more information, including websites. (Please note, however, that we have no control over most of these websites.)

A glossary of abbreviations and symbols used is given below, and **an index** of places and people can be found towards the end of the book. **NB** The spelling of place names can vary considerably, as a result of Breton names having been written phonetically by French speakers, and vice versa. Lock names particularly will be found to have various forms.

One final point: there is no reason to limit walking the canal to the summer season. The towpath makes an accessible route at any time of the year and there is much of interest to see along the way, even in the depths of winter! May and October are perhaps the best choices for appreciating the natural, unspoilt world of the canal.

GLOSSARY

bief . . . . cut channel

bief de partage . . . . cut channel at highest point (watershed)

bourg . . . . village with facilities

chaland . . . . barge, lighter

chemin de halage . . . . towpath

chômage . . . . maintenance period (water drained)

contre-halage . . . .path on opposite side of the canal to the towpath

écluse . . . . lock

éclusier . . . . lock-keeper

gîte d'étape . . . . hostel

GR . . . . long distance footpath

mairie . . . . town hall

passerelle . . . . pedestrian bridge

péniche . . . . . . motorised version of *chaland*

pont . . . . bridge

rigole . . . . feeder channel

sentier . . . . footpath

TO . . . . Tourist Office

VTC   *vélo tout chemin* (hybrid bike)

VTT *vélo tout terrain* (mountain bike)

Note on maps

Because the canal is constantly changing direction, following it in the book can sometimes be confusing: it helps to make use of the spiral binding to view pages one at a time.

All the numbered maps of the canal between Lock 2 Quiheix and 237 Guily Glas are drawn to the same scale.

French IGN maps (1:25000) in the Série Bleue are available for all parts of the canal's course, although not all are up-to-date in terms of footpaths.

Map Symbols

- - - - towpath

|►| lock (arrow in direction of flow)

━━ road bridge

━━ railway bridge

⇒✕⇐ level crossing

━━ footbridge

╅╆ suspension bridge

○ road access to towpath, parking possible

P parking provided

✳ viewpoint/belvedere

+ chapel

⚲ church

🞩 picnic table(s)

🔲 seat

Δ monument

📶 VTT circuit

⑰ cycle ride (arrow for direction of circuit, here anti-clockwise)

🚶 walk circuit

GR380 long distance footpath

GRADING AND COLOUR CODING OF CYCLE CIRCUITS

easy (green) = fairly level, roads and/or well-maintained tracks

medium (blue) = some hills and possibly earth tracks

energetic (red) = very up and down (possibility of poor surfaces at the limit of VTC capability)

difficult (black) = you probably need a mountain-bike (VTT)

GRADING OF VTT/MOUNTAIN BIKE ROUTES - colour coded:

green = family (*famille*)

blue = leisure (*loisir*)

red = sport (*sportif*)

black = extreme (*extrème*)

SIGNS AND WAYMARKS

Generally, cycle routes are well signed, although circuits are often signed in one direction only. On the few occasions when there appears to be a lack of signs, the rule that usually holds good is to follow the road you are on. (This also applies where there is a sign but it doesn't clearly indicate any direction.)

Occasionally a signed route will vary from the published one. This might be the result of problems occurring after the route has been published, so in these circumstances it is best to follow the signs rather than printed information.

PLEASE NOTE

All distances given are approximate.

Opening hours of restaurants, shops, etc. often differ from those advertised and cannot be absolutely relied upon. On Mondays many establishments are likely to be shut, especially in small villages.

On the accommodation, refreshments and provisions pages (see p.112), a selection with varied price ranges is provided. Local tourist offices may be able to supply details of other establishments.

Péniches in the port at Redon

Musée de la Batellerie

Warehouse at Rohan

INTRODUCTION

The Nantes-Brest canal, for walking purposes, does not really start in Nantes nor end in Brest, but the original plan had the intention of linking these places by an internal route across Brittany. 18th century English harassment and blockades of the Breton coasts – particularly the Rade de Brest – made secure navigational routes desirable for both military and commercial purposes. Today the towpath (*chemin de halage*) starts at Lock 2, Quiheix, near Nort-sur-Erdre and provides a continuous route to Guily Glas in Finistère about 350 kms to the west. The canal has two 'faces': firstly that of the seven canalised rivers making up most of its course, and secondly the artificial man-made sections linking the major river valleys. It is largely the first of these aspects that gives the canal such a striking diversity of character and atmosphere along its full length.

Proposals

From earliest times in Brittany transport by water was used extensively for transferring goods either via the coast or up and down large rivers such as the Vilaine and the Aulne. Inland towns like Redon, Quimper and Landerneau were

11

vibrant river ports, capable of handling large three-masted sailing ships.

There was little in the way of a road network, and such routes that were in regular use were often impassable in winter. A need existed for improved movement of goods internally, particularly for the development of agriculture in central Brittany.

Attempts at canal construction were taking place in Brittany as early as the mid-16th century, with a series of short-lived locks on the Vilaine south of Rennes. Another scheme to canalise the Aulne in Finistère foundered through lack of finance in the early 17th century.

In 1746 François-Joseph de Kersauson presented extensive proposals for the canalisation of Brittany to the governing body, the *États de Bretagne*. His ambitious schemes included linking the Rance and Vilaine (from which Rennes in particular would benefit), the Loire and Vilaine, and the Blavet and Oust. Nearly twenty years later, de Kersauson added the suggestion of joining the Blavet and the Aulne.

These ideas came at a time when the English fleet was wreaking havoc around the Breton coastline - Breton ports were blockaded during the war of the Austrian succession around 1744, and fifteen years later the French fleet suffered a disastrous defeat - subject of the song, Heart of Oak, by David Garrick - off the Atlantic coast near Brest. English and French imperial ambitions and commercial imperatives came constantly into bloody conflict at this time.

In 1780, during the American Wars of Independence, the Breton coast was once more beset by the English fleet and the importance of an internal supply line between the military arsenals at Brest, Lorient and Indret (near Nantes) was again evident.

The consequence of constructing a canal network would be beneficial to industry and commerce, as well as strategically significant. With Redon and St-Malo also linked by canal, a great increase in trade was possible along a north-

EXTRAIT

DES REGISTRES DU GREFFE

DES ETATS DE BRETAGNE,

TENUS A RENNES.

Du Mercredi 19 Janvier 1783.

Monseigneur L'EVÊQUE DE RENNES.
Monseigneur le Comte DE BERTHOU DE LA VIOLAYE.
Monsieur LE SÉNÉCHAL DE RENNES.

LES Etats délibérant sur le rapport de la Commission nom-
mée le 18 de ce mois, pour l'examen du Mémoire de M.
DE PIRÉ, fils, contenant deux objets principaux, l'un concer-
nant l'Etablissement d'un Port de Roi à Saint Malo, l'autre,
relatif aux Canaux à ouvrir, à l'effet de réunir Angers à
A

Musée de la Batellerie

south route across Brittany, and similar traffic from east to west would also open up the impoverished hinterland of Brittany to new economic and cultural influences.

In 1783 a commission was set up by the *États de Bretagne*. A map of two proposed routes (Nantes/Brest and the Rance/Vilaine link) was put to the king, Louis XVI, in 1784 and in the following February members of the *Académie Royale* presented a detailed proposal for joining rivers to make a navigable route right across Brittany.

Decisions

After the French Revolution, the *États de Bretagne* was dissolved and decision-making came from central government. Napoleon's wars of empire brought further pressures to the Breton coasts and enhanced the importance of the work of the arsenals for arming and equipping French ships. Linking the arsenals of Lorient and Brest with those of Nantes and St-Malo became a priority.

The official go-ahead for the canal came in 1804, with the *Ponts et Chaussées* administrative body made responsible for the work. Chief Engineer Guy Boussel, who had already worked on the 1780s scheme, was charged with the feasibility studies for the Nantes-Brest route. One surprising outcome of these was the decision to link the Oust and Blavet via Rohan/Pontivy rather than the apparently easier earlier proposal via Bieuzy and Bocneuf. The designation of Pontivy, now called Napoleonville, as a military centre and Breton showpiece for the new regime, presumably accounted for this.

Canalisation of the Blavet to link Pontivy and Lorient was also authorised at this time, as well as work on the Ille-et-Rance stretch that would link St-Malo to the south coast.

The Task

The scope of the Nantes-Brest canal project was vast: to connect four major river valleys - the Loire, the Vilaine, the Blavet and the Aulne. In effect, only 20% of the length of the canal is artificial, with these sections linking the rivers utilised - the Erdre, Isac, Oust, Blavet, Doré, Kergoat, Hyères and Aulne. A lack of proper maps made the engineers' task even harder, but the work involved scaling heights between river basins, cutting through Brittany's ubiquitous granite and steering a firm course through the marshland of the *marais*.

In addition to these Herculean engineering feats, a series of 237 locks was required, enabling the canal to rise and fall between river valleys, as well as a secure towpath and the reservoirs and feeder streams (*rigoles*) needed to supply water to the artificial sections of the canal. At its highest point (Glomel in Côtes d'Armor) the canal rose to 184m above sea level. When considering the millions of cubic metres of earth and rubble to be shifted, it's worth remembering that all the main work of digging, clearing and reinforcing was effected by hand with basic tools.

In addition to the canal itself, lock-houses, bridges (including the new technique of *ponts metalliques suspendus*), *passerelles* and supply roads were also needed.

In the end, the canal cost approximately 60,000,000 francs (of the mid 19th century), which translates into well over 150 millions euros in today's figures.

Progress

Work began in 1806 on the canalisation of the Aulne between Port Launay and Pont Triffen. In 1811 the first lock at Port-Launay was opened by the Prefect of Finistère with great

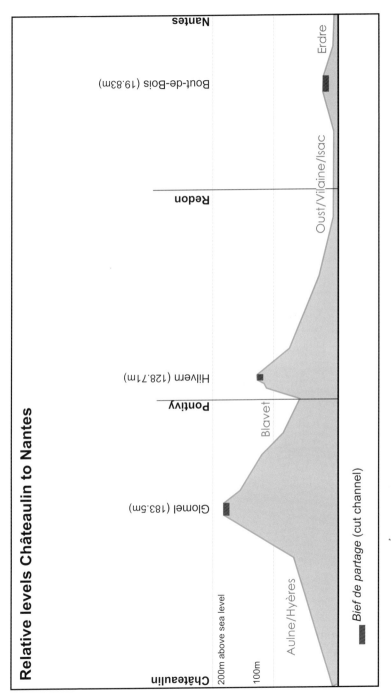

Relative levels Châteaulin to Nantes

Châteaulin

200m above sea level

100m

Glomel (183.5m)

Aulne/Hyères

Pontivy

Blavet

Hilvern (128.71m)

Redon

Oust/Vilaine/Isac

Bout-de-Bois (19.83m)

Erdre

Nantes

Bief de partage (cut channel)

ceremony – 'a new monument to the glory and grandeur of the great Napoleon'. From 1810 construction started at the other end in Nantes. Four years later the project came to a halt with Napoleon's fall from grace.

It was taken up again in 1822 when the *Compagnie des Canaux de Bretagne* was formed. Work then began on new sites in Côtes du Nord (now Côtes d'Armor) and Morbihan too. It was envisaged that completion would require ten years at a cost of 30 million francs – the reality was double that (and commercial usage never came near to justifying such figures).

The Duchess of Berry laid the first stone of the first lock in

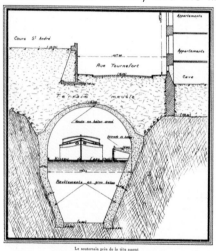

Nantes on 29 June 1828, hence the name 'écluse de Madame'. (This no longer exists, as a tunnel now houses the Erdre at that point - today the *écluse maritime St-Felix* is the first of the canal.)

The Blavet canal by contrast was finished relatively quickly by 1826, with a total of 28 locks, whilst that of the Ille-et-Rance opened in May 1832.

Musée de la Batellerie
Cross-section of the tunnel under Nantes

Construction

Providing the linking sections of the canal (*biefs de partage*) with adequate and consistent water supply required the use of reservoirs and connecting feeder streams (*rigoles*). A large amount of water - about 300m³ - was lost each time a boat passed through a lock, and there was also leakage into the surrounding farmland. Often the water to replenish these losses was brought from a considerable distance.

At Bout-de-Bois (see p.40), for example, where an 8km

section was needed to connect the Erdre and the Isac rivers, the *rigole* covered 22kms from the reservoir at Vioreau in its contour-dictated course. It was constructed between 1812 and 1814 by 1200 prisoners at the Jarriais camp, who returned to Spain after the fall of the empire and Napoleon's downfall.

In theory the *rigoles* needed some elementary lining of sedimentary clay mixed with straw to prevent wholesale leakage. At Hilvern, the *rigole* from the reservoir at Bosméléac takes an astonishing 64kms of meanders to reach its destination (see p.69), and on its initial test when filled in 1836, little water actually made it as far as the canal.

Another major feat was the construction of the towpath (*chemin de halage*). There was none from Nantes up the Erdre, despite a proposal of 1811 for the work, so the use of sail or tug was necessary up to Quiheix, just off the river 20kms north.

The towpath was about 2m wide, of earth or gravel, and raised to avoid flooding, almost like a dyke in places between the canal and the *marais*. A ditch (*contre-both*) to the side of the towpath provided capacity for streams from the river basin as well as water draining from fields on both sides.

Locks

Locks were essential to enable boats to move up and down the canal as water levels changed. On the steepest stretches, whole ladders of locks were required: on the connecting link between the Oust and the Blavet, for example, there are 12 in 1.6kms at Le Roz (see p.70).

Exceptionally firm foundations were needed for the locks, and 24 hour pumping had to be in place during their construction. Often stakes of water-resistant wood which would not rot, such as chestnut, were laid, followed by a layer of stones and cement before blocks of granite were used for the lock itself. These blocks were joined by mortice and tenon joints.

The lock gates were made of oak and metal - (cont.p.20)

A typical lock (*écluse*)

1. canal upstream (*bief amont*)
2. canal downstream (*bief aval*)
3. lock (*sas*)
4. lock gate (*porte*)

5. weir (*barrage*)
6. footbridge (*passerelle*)
7. chute
8. lock-keeper's cottage (maison éclusière)

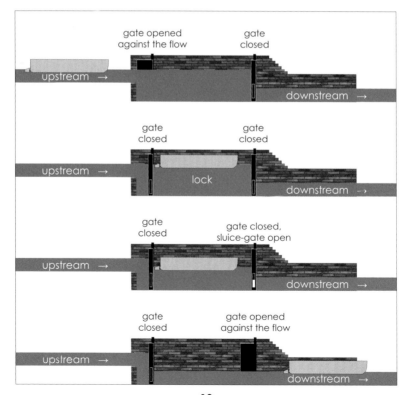

Closing the gates prior to filling the lock

Old oak gate with iron sluice-gate

Old oak gates still in place

IL EST FORMELLEMENT INTERDIT
DE LAISSER L'ÉCLUSE PLEINE
DE LAISSER DESCENDRE LES CRICS
SANS L'AIDE DE LA MANIVELLE

'It is forbidden to leave the lock full or to let the ratchet drop without using the cranked handle'

'V' shaped gates held closed by the weight of water

A silt-guard wall keeps the lock entrance clear of debris from the river

- now steel, and rested in a V-shape when closed to withstand the pressure of the water. A trap in the bottom of each gate could be raised or lowered to let water in and out of the lock. The lock-keeper opened the traps by hand with the help of *manivelles* (cranked handle). Some locks in the eastern section of the canal have motorised movements today.

The standard dimensions of a lock were 25.7m long, 4.7m wide and a depth of about 4m. The barrage drop was usually around 2.4m. In places chutes to act as fish ladders were also included. Between 1870 and 1890 improvements were made to locks to increase the speed of transport via the canal.

Lock-keeper and his family

Musée de la Batellerie

Lock-houses

Not all locks had lock-houses attached, as in a line of closely spaced locks, one man could manage several. The lock-houses were often built on unstable foundations, unsurprisingly given their position, and humidity was a frequent problem. The ground floor was usually raised by a few steps as a precaution against flooding, which was a regular hazard.

The houses were built to a standard pattern, which varied a

little from area to area. Essentially they were very basic and purely functional. Jean-Marie de Silguy, later a distinguished patron of the arts in Quimper, designed one at Châteaulin in 1923, whilst a humble engineer of the *Ponts et Chaussées*. Before the 1930s many were without toilets or water, one result of their isolated locations. A small piece of land for growing vegetables was attached to the lock-house, and often a stable where horses pulling the boats could stay overnight.

The lock-keeper was an employee of the *Administration des Ponts et Chaussées*. In addition to managing the lock for the passage of boats, he also had to maintain the banks and surrounding area.

Manpower and Working Conditions

Shortage of workers for construction of a canal on this scale was an ongoing problem.

Initially where local labour was employed by contractors, especially in Finistère, the project was welcomed, but in areas of shortage or lack of takers because of low wages, other solutions were necessary. Hired labourers were paid miserably at barely subsistence level. It was so hard to recruit workers that some were brought in from as far afield as the Auvergne and Limousin. A decree of 1811 made it possible for prisoners of war to be used – these were not in short supply.

Near Saffré in Loire-Atlantique a camp was built to house Spanish prisoners working on the section joining the Erdre and the Isac rivers (see p.40). In Côtes d'Armor there was another camp at Glomel (see p.84-5) for prisoners (*bagnards*) from gaols in Brest (deserters from the Spanish Wars), Belle-Île and Belle-Croix who laboured for nearly ten years on cutting the *Grande Tranchée*, an extraordinary feat of endurance.

Canal construction work was unremitting and arduous, often in damp, humid and insalubrious conditions. Stone and soil were carried to and from sites on men's backs, and the constant pumping and bailing out of water essential to lock construction was done by hand.

Long hours and poor nutrition compounded the misery. The prisoners' food consisted of bread, meat, dried vegetables and wine (not enough of the latter, according to a doctor who attended one of the camps). Disease was rife: the threat of epidemics due to the close proximity of living conditions hung over the work-camps.

Some prisoners were buried where they fell on the banks of the canal as local communities refused to allow access to their cemeteries for these men.

Many workers died in accidents, such as those involving the explosives used to clear rock. Broken health from the extreme physical taxation of the task accounted for many further deaths.

In Finistère a labourer died at lock Steréon in 1824 and there was another fatal accident at lock Bizernic near Châteauneuf two years later. Families received no compensation in these circumstances.

Opening

The canal from Nantes to Redon was fully operational in November 1833 and the first boat left Nantes for St-Malo on 19th January 1834 with a cargo of iron, reaching its destination on 3rd February. The Finistère stretch of the canal, a length of 81kms, opened the following year, but it was not until 1842 that the Nantes-Brest canal was navigable in its entirety. In 1858 an inauguration ceremony by Napoleon III, on a state visit to Brittany, took place at Guily Glas, the westernmost lock.

Transport

Boats could carry much greater loads than carts, and there were not the same time pressures for transport then as today. The wooden *chalands nantais*, made from oak, were the main type of boats on the canal initially, although metal versions became more common later in the century. An early example was the *Jeanne d'Arc*, built in 1850 for Yves

Vigouroux of Port Launay, and *Victor* (whose interesting story can be found on p.93), built in Nantes in 1893 for Nicolas le Page.

In 1917, lack of wood and skilled workers meant *chalands* were constructed of *béton armé* (reinforced concrete), but in fact wooden ones were more flexible and stronger. After WWI, motorised *péniches* were gradually introduced. The use of horses became less and less common.

The boats were often worked by the owner (*marinier*) with the aid of his spouse. They would live and work on the boat, whilst children either joined in or stayed with relatives to ensure regular schooling. It was an itinerant lifestyle, with the boat – about 26m long and 4.6m wide - the sole focus of family, society and livelihood. Sometimes another worker, a *matelot*, was part of the team.

Initially a man might pull his own boat before the purchase of a horse, and then two people were sufficient to work – one on deck and one on the towpath to manage the horse. The hauling rope was attached at the middle or front of the boat, and the horse's equipment consisted of a collar, traces and a metal bar.

When two boats wanted to pass, that moving with the current had priority: the horse of the other boat was un-

Musée de la Batellerie

harnessed by the *matelot* (assistant) and the *marinier* tied up the boat. The horse was then re-harnessed when the other boat had passed.

A horse-drawn boat could cover up to 25kms a day, but with motorisation, over 100km was possible.

The movement and transactions of boats were carefully monitored. A *carnet de route* had to be filled in and carried at all times. Finistère police regulations issued in 1897 concerning canal transport cover topics like the height and width of boats, lighting, personnel (one *marinier* to be on board at all times) and the management of horses on the towpath. A list of forbidden behaviour includes throwing things into the canal!

Movement on the canal could be hazardous. A report from the *Ouest-France* newspaper in February 1966 describes the mishap which befell the *péniche Laborieux*, owned by M. Lelièvre. A combination of mist, dark and flooding marooned it in a field near Guenrouet. It took the aid of ten other boats and their crews to gently pull it back into the canal - because '*on ne remue pas 40 tonnes comme un fetu du paille*'!

Usage

Between 1836 and 1856, the first twenty years of the canal, the average tonnage was 10,000, although this increased to 40,000 by 1860, thanks to an official decision to build 62 iron *péniches* for transporting oil between Nantes and Brest. This proved an expensive experiment which stopped after a few years.

The costs of using the Nantes-Brest canal were always higher than canals in other parts of France. This reflected the enormous costs of the construction through that terrain, but the users of the canal were hardly running their boats at great profit to start with. In fact, the most efficient internal water transport was within one river basin, avoiding the delays of a series of locks.

The heyday of the canal was the last ten years of the 19th century and up until the outbreak of war in 1914, a period when as many as 800 boats were active along the canal. The cost of transporting heavy goods by railway was still high at this time, and by now the infrastructure necessary for greater efficiency along the canal had been developed, with improved design of boats and locks, and the establishment of many commercial associations.

Cargoes

Essentially traffic on the canal was agricultural rather than industrial.

A major benefit was the importation of fertilisers (*engrais*) to improve the often poor and acidic soil of central Brittany. Lime was originally used in construction work, but mid-18th century research led to an understanding of its benefits for agriculture. Lime, sand and marl were all brought in by boat and played a vital role in increasing the yield of crops.

Wood was the main load, either moved locally for fuel, or transported to the many forges of the interior, and to large cities like Nantes, Brest and Lorient. Slate and stone for construction purposes were also common cargoes, especially as quarry enterprises developed in Finistère (see p.91). Iron was carried to and from the forges, such as Les Forges des Salles near Bon Repos.

Grains (*blé noir, froment, avoines*) - were another major export, whilst items of *épicerie* like wine, oil, salt, soap, etc. were brought in from Nantes in large quantities.

As an example, here are the loads of *Le Pourquoi-Pas* in 1930-1:

- 9 Dec - 4 Jan: (empty Lochrist to Pontivy) grains from Pontivy to Nantes
- 4 - 29 Jan: divers goods Nantes to Pontivy
- 29 Jan - 21 Feb: grains Pontivy to Nantes
- 21 Feb - 16 March: (empty Nantes to Montjean) lime from Montjean to Josselin
- 16 - 25 March: (empty Josselin to Bellions) stone from Bellions to St-Clair
- 25 March -11 April: sand from Nantes to Rennes
- 11 - 22 April: wood from Rennes to Nantes

Maintenance

The canal has always required regular maintenance, and on the artificial sections, this has meant periods of *chômage*, when the water is drained to allow access to the bed, banks and substructure. On river sections, clearing of weeds and debris is also an ongoing task. Locks inevitably require remedial work on a consistent basis to ensure their smooth functioning. When the canal was in commercial use, this was generally in the summer and no transport would be possible for some weeks; today, out of season when pleasure craft are infrequent is more common. There is also constant need for cutting and managing vegetation along the entire route.

Lac de Guerlédan used to be drained every ten years for barrage maintenance, and the ghostly outlines of submerged locks and lock-houses can be seen.

Decline

The development of the railway in Brittany came hard on the heels of the completed canal. In terms of speed and efficiency, there was no competition, although it took a while before relative costs and transport links swung the balance decidedly in favour of the train.

The first World War brought an end to the canal's brief heyday. During this time, boats were requisitioned for war and many Bretons were at the fronts fighting. The vitality of central Brittany was sapped decisively by the war years and their grim legacy. In the post-war period lorry transport began to develop significantly.

In 1919 an article by Henri Quilgars mourned the decline of the canal network in Brittany, arguing that it was just as essential for economic development as the railways, and citing the success of German canals as an example. His arguments highlight the main weaknesses: the canals were too localized and not connected to the rest of France (due to the capriciousness and unmanageability of the Loire); transport was inefficient and not properly organized, with boats often travelling empty. Improvements were essential to internal ports like Redon and better links with railway stations vital, as well as development of industrial areas around the canal. He urged long-term thinking and the development of the canal network for the future. '*Relier Brest au Rhin, c'est ne pas un rêve, c'est une question de vie nationale!*' Such a link was possible through Laval, Le Mans and the Marne, but he bemoaned the lack of vision and initiative that looked to local interests only.

Shortly after this article was published, the death-knell of the canal sounded.

In 1923 permission was granted for the SGE (*Société générale d'entreprise*) to manage the canal between Bon Repos and Guerlédan. Despite the protests of *bateliers*, whose livelihood was threatened with extinction, 12 kilometres of the Blavet valley were flooded to create Lac de Guerlédan and a means of generating electric power. The lake engulfed 400 hectares of woodland, houses, 18 locks and lock-keepers cottages.

A ladder of locks was mooted, to keep through navigation feasible, but estimated costs soon put a stop to that idea: canal trade was simply not great enough to justify such investment. In September 1930 the barrage and hydroelectric station were opened: the canal was effectively severed once and for all in central Brittany.

After 1936, with workers rights more of an issue, there were limits on the working hours of lock-keepers, so travel at night or during the midday period was impossible. As all delays added to the costs of transporting goods, this was another nail in the canal's commercial coffin.

Boats were again requisitioned during WWII, and although trade continued in both halves of the canal, the writing was on the wall for its commercial viability. In 1977, the last working *péniche*, *Le Mistral*, left its last cargo of sand at Saint-Congard in Morbihan.

Conclusions

Ultimately the canal was too slow and therefore relatively too expensive to compete as economic imperatives speeded up and rail/road links improved dramatically. It was still quicker to take grain from Finistère by canal to Port Launay and then round the coast to Nantes! The 'blue road' route was also unreliable, with periods of *chômage* and adverse weather conditions, both drought and flood. Lack of water brought things to a halt in 1921/2, for example, and even in 1995 flooding made navigation on the Aulne impossible – hence the new barrage (2006) at Guily Glas.

But despite the ultimate (and predictable) economic failure, usage of the canal did open up previously isolated and poor areas of central Brittany to the benefits of commercial possibility and general communication with the outside world.

Leisure Resource

Today the canal is managed by various departmental bodies as a leisure and educational resource. There is no one unified strategy of development but the Association Canaux de Bretagne, based in Rennes, is a focal point for many initiatives. Other local associations promote the heritage and history of all the canals in Brittany and encourage their leisure usage.

Other bodies, such as SMATAH in Finistère, have created *Maisons du Canal*, situated in lock-houses, which house exhibitions and information centres for diverse aspects of canal culture and history. These include flora (at Lock 203, Kergoat), fauna (Lock 232 Aulne) and the life of a lock-keeper (Lock 224 Rosvéguen). In the summer season, demonstrations of canal-related practices, such as the horse-drawn *chaland* - are held all along the canal.

Apart from the towpath itself and the *contre-halage* on the opposte bank, many connecting footpaths (*sentiers*) facilitate circular walks in the surrounding countryside, and cycling and kayaking are other popular ways of exploiting the canal, in addition to the pleasure boats that still enjoy the changing landscape at a leisurely pace. The eastern section, particularly from Nantes to Rohan is the most used part of the canal today.

There is no doubt that the full route deserves to be better used, throughout the year, especially by walkers.

Loire-Atlantique

The canal runs through Loire-Atlantique from Nantes to Redon. Historically this region was part of Brittany, with Nantes the old ducal capital from the time of Alain Barbetorte in the 10th century. During the German occupation of WWII, the Vichy government separated Nantes and the surrounding territory as an administrative and economic entity called Loire-Inférieure. In 1957 this became Loire-Atlantique, a region of Pays de la Loire.

For this reason, the canal has acquired a symbolic historic and political significance as it retains the link with this former part of Brittany. The Association 'Le Canal de l'Unité' promotes this aspect of the canal and an annual celebration of Breton heritage and identity.

Geographically the canal in Loire Atlantique passes mainly through what is by and large a flat and watery terrain, with extensive *marais* (marshes) to both sides of the canal. This limits the number of settlements in the vicinity, and locks are relatively few and far between up to Redon. The countryside is mostly open and unremarkable, although there are some exceptions, with stretches of attractive scenery between Blain and Guenrouet.

It is not an area especially well served for accommodation near the canal, so planning and pre-booking are advised.

Morbihan

Shortly after Redon, and entering the department of Morbihan, the canal passes through the striking 'gateway' of *falaises* as the Oust approaches the Île aux Pies. There is certainly some beautiful scenery to be enjoyed as the canal, mainly following the river course, wends its way up to Malestroit and then Josselin, two exceptionally attractive historic towns with much of interest to offer the passing traveller. The route is studded with oases of tranquillity like Montertelot, offering enticement to rest and repose, and constant changes of view and perspective alongside the wide sweet-flowing Oust. Past Rohan, the quiet calm of the Forêt de Branguily provides a different type of walking experience, with the canal including a chain of lakes between locks and delapidated lock-houses. This practical and scenic feature is repeated on the final stretch to Pontivy, which includes the engineering feat of a ladder of twelve locks (échelle de Roz) in a serene and verdant environment. After the Napoleonic creation of Pontivy (around a fine medieval quarter and château), the neglected canal moves sadly north towards its demise at the barrage of Lac de Guerlédan.

Côtes d'Armor

Lac de Guerlédan with its wooded shores, swimming beaches and recreational facilities is a major focus for tourist activity in this department, but elsewhere the canal provides a quiet and relaxing form of exercise. The creation of the lake and its barrage put an end to through boating traffic on the canal, and the most neglected parts of this great waterway lie in Côtes d'Armor. This is not to say that the will for regeneration is lacking, however, and there are certainly some exceptionally pretty and historically interesting places along the way. The Abbey of Bon Repos is an early example, and the double-lock of Coatnatous in its idyllic setting followed by the remarkable Grande Tranchée makes for a most satisfying day's walk later on. The latter (unsurprisingly given the human toil and suffering involved in its creation) can seem melancholy and sombre even on a bright summer's day! It is this variation in tone and atmosphere, so characteristic of the canal, that is most evident in these sections.

There are no towns on the route past Gouarec, just an essentially rural ramble occasionally punctuated by main road crossings.

Finistère

In Finistère walking the canal is to follow the flow of the water all the way to the end. It is a quiet, verdant route, where the deep silence characteristic of the towpath here is rarely disturbed by traffic or agrarian/industrial noise. The Aulne gets increasingly impressive as it crosses the department, flowing under the old bridge below the hill-town of Châteauneuf-du-Faou, with the pink stone of the 'château rose' on the opposite hillside also a memorable sight. It then takes a series of huge looping bends towards Châteaulin, where the broad river runs right through the centre of the town. Along the way are frequent remnants of the many quarries that sprang up to exploit the transportation potential of the canal in its heyday, with Port Launay a centre of exports to the wider world. Modern technology has brought a state-of-the-art barrage to Guily Glas, where the canal ends at Lock 237, but those who pursue the final objective of the Rade de Brest can pick up the free-flowing Aulne beyond this point with the reward of a superb walk from the suspension bridge of Pont de Térénez through the Forêt de Landévennec to the exceptional site of its ancient abbey.

NANTES

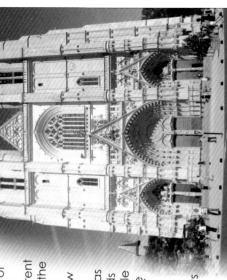

Nantes is situated on the banks of the Loire at the confluence with the rivers Erdre and Sèvre. A natural commercial centre, it was originally the port and settlement of the Celtic Namnetes tribe. Felix, bishop from 549-582, instigated works to improve the growing city's navigation: the first lock of the Nantes-Brest canal today is named after him. In 843 Nantes was sacked by Vikings who slaughtered the inhabitants and burnt down the cathedral. For a time, after a second raid, they held the city until Alain Barbetorte, duke of Brittany, retook Nantes and made it his capital. The current ducal château was built in the 15th century and was the

Château of the dukes of Brittany

birthplace of Anne de Bretagne, last ruler of an independent Brittany. It now houses an excellent history museum.

Nantes' greatest commercial prosperity came in the 18th century and was largely based on the slave trade. Ships went first to Africa with cheap goods to exchange for slaves who were then transported to the West Indies for sale as labour. Sugar and coffee were then brought back to the home port. The exceptional architecture of the merchants' houses on the île Feydeau reflects the lucrative earnings of this period. In more modern times, the city became a renowned centre of ship-building.

In the bloody aftermath of the French Revolution, the Terror had its effects in Nantes where the governor Carrier killed thousands of royalists between October 1793 and February 1794 by hideous drownings in the Loire.

Originally the first lock of the canal was the Ecluse de Madame, so-called as it was officially opened by the Duchess of Berry in 1828, although the name changed when she was arrested a few years later. This lock was lost in the 1930s, when the Erdre was diverted through a tunnel from the Canal St-Felix. The Ecluse Maritime St-Felix thus became the first lock of the Nantes-Brest Canal. The old course of the Erdre is marked by the *Cours de 50 Otages*.

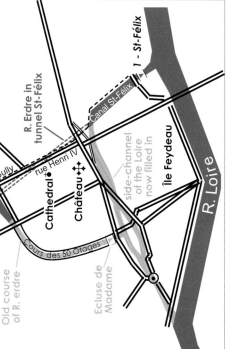

Ecluse maritime St-Félix

In 1930, under the Dawes plan of War Reparations, the German firm Carl Brandt of Düsseldorf was involved in the construction of the tunnel. Their engineer Karl Hotz was in Nantes from 1930-1933. In 1940 he returned as a *Feld Kommandant* and was assassinated by a member of the Resistance in 1941. In reprisal 50 hostages were shot. As a memorial the road over the old course of the Erdre is called 'Cours des 50 Otages'.

From NANTES to Quiheix

It is not possible to walk directly up the Erdre from Nantes to the start of the canal proper at Quiheix, as much of the riverside land is privately owned.

The best route starts from Saint-Felix, the first lock off the Loire, and follows the river through its tunnel for a short way before emerging to cross towards the Château. Continue straight ahead to the right of the château for about 500m to rejoin the Erdre, and stay on the same side to follow it northwards as far as Port Breton. An inland passage through private estates is then signed as far as the road bridge crossing to Sucé-sur-Erdre.

For accommodation in Nantes: Tourist Office
08 92 46 40 44
00 33 272 640 479 (from outside France)
www.nantes-tourisme.com

It is also possible to follow a footpath up the other side of the Erdre (right bank) past Le Port Barbe and the Château de la Desnerie to La-Chapelle-sur-Erdre, after which it takes a more inland route to Sucé-sur-Erdre.

Cyclists can follow the D69 (right bank) to Sucé-sur-Erdre, then continue north on this same road, turning right to the canal just before the junction with the D26 (see map on p.37).

La Chapelle-
sur-Erdre

N

1km

A11

Pont de la
Beaujoire

NANTES

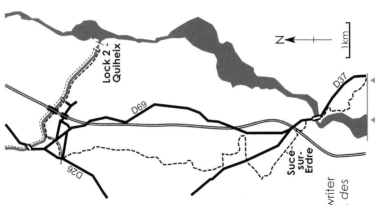

From Sucé-sur-Erdre, a cross-country walk reaches the D26 at Le Pas Chevalier: here turn right after the bridge, and cross straight over the D69 to reach the canal. At the canal turn right and follow it for 2.5 kms to the *Ecluse de Quiheix* and the start of the canal's westward journey. Cross over the lock to the towpath on the other side.

For accommodation in Sucé-sur-Erdre:

see Map 1 and p.50

Entrance to the canal at Quiheix

Admirers of the Erdre include King François 1 in the 16th century, and the writer Flaubert in 1847 , who described this *'gentille rivière avec des jolis aspects, des arbres dans le gout des vielles gravures du XVIIIé siècle.'*

MAP 1

Ecluse 2 – Quiheix

Technically the second lock of the canal (first in Nantes), this is the natural starting place for a walk along the towpath, the first section of canal proper as it turns westwards from the Erdre, a river described by François I as *'la plus belle rivière de France'*. Toilets and information here.

ACCOMMODATION & SERVICES • see page 112

Nort-sur-Erdre Acc 1,2,3,5, 6. Ref Pro
5kms

D26

Pont de Vive Eve

2

The Erdre

Lock 2. Quiheix

wc

22kms

see p.102

17

GR380

2

Sucé-sur-Erdre Acc 4. Ref Pro

D69

N

500m

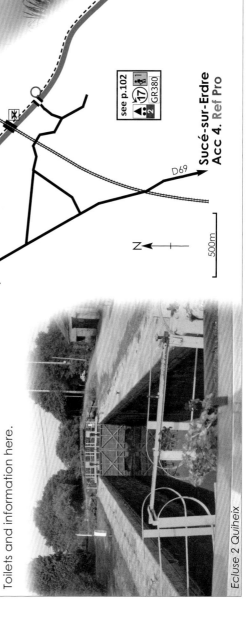

Ecluse 2 Quiheix

Nort-sur-Erdre Acc 1.2.3.5. ⛺ 6. Ref Pro

(TO – 02 51 12 60 74 / www.nort-sur-erdre.fr)

This town, with a full range of services, is three kilometres from the nearest section of canal, and six from the lock at Quiheix, where most walkers begin their journey. There is a busy pleasure port, Le Bassin, and boats can be hired for cruising on the Erdre or canal.

The 19th century neogothic church of St Christopher contains a fine display of stained glass of the period; it has no bell-tower, relying on one already existing from an earlier edifice a little distance away. The town celebrates its apple festival, *Fête de la Pomme*, each year on the last Friday of September.

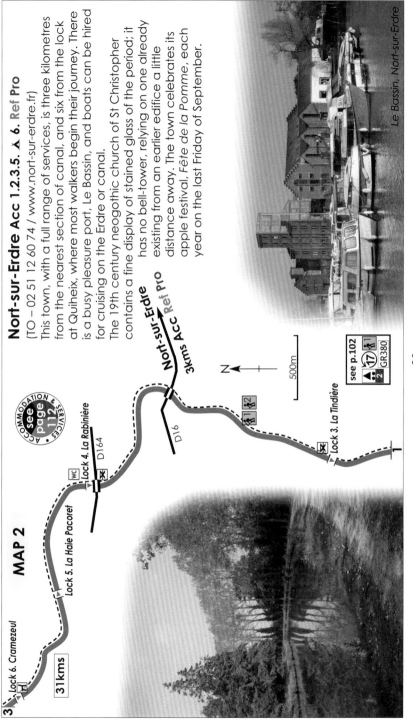

MAP 2

Lock 6. Cramezeul

31kms

Lock 5. La Haie Pacoret

Lock 4. La Rabinière

WC

D164

Nort-sur-Erdre
Acc Ref Pro

3kms Nort-sur-Erdre

D16

N

500m

Lock 3. La Tindière

see p.102

17

2

GR380

Le Bassin, Nort-sur-Erdre

39

MAP 3

Le Camp

In 1812, Spanish prisoners of war were used to construct the *bief de partage* of Bout-de-Bois, and housed in a camp at Jarriais in the commune of Saffré. After Napoleon's downfall in 1814, the camp was closed and the prisoners released to make their way home. Work began again in 1822 with free labour.

Aqueduct - rigole de Vioreau

The *Rigole* here covers a distance of 22 kms from its feeder reservoir at Vioreau. Its construction involved four arched aqueducts and a 600m underground section.

Lock 7 - Pas d'Héric

32kms

N

500m

Rigole de Vioreau

Saffré

D39

see p.102

Le Camp

R. Isac

Rigole de Vioreau

see page 112
ACCOMMODATION & SERVICES

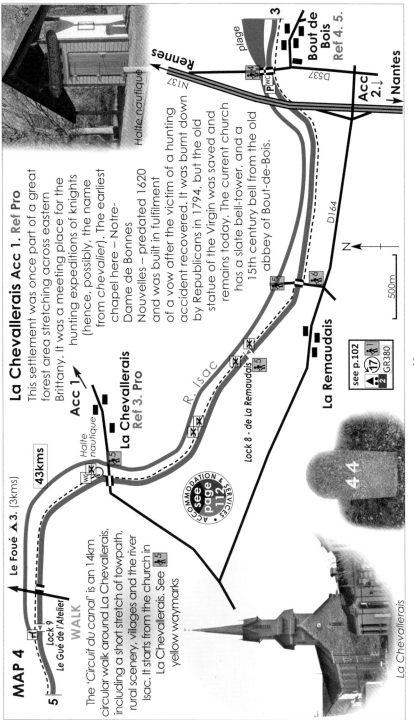

MAP 4

WALK

The 'Circuit du canal' is an 14km circular walk around La Chevallerais, including a short stretch of towpath, rural scenery, villages and the river Isac. It starts from the church in La Chevallerais. See yellow waymarks

Le Foué ⚑ 3. (3kms)

43kms

Lock 9
Le Gué de l'Atelier

Acc 1

Halte nautique

La Chevallerais
Ref 3. Pro

R. Isac

Lock 8 - de La Remaudais

ACCOMMODATION & SERVICES
see page 112

La Remaudais

La Chevallerais Acc 1. Ref Pro

This settlement was once part of a great forest area stretching across eastern Brittany. It was a meeting place for the hunting expeditions of knights (hence, possibly, the name from *chevalier*). The earliest chapel here – Notre-Dame de Bonnes Nouvelles – predated 1620 and was built in fulfilment of a vow after the victim of a hunting accident recovered. It was burnt down by Republicans in 1794, but the old statue of the Virgin was saved and remains today. The current church has a slate bell-tower, and a 15th century bell from the old abbey of Bout-de-Bois.

Halte nautique

Rennes

N137

P WC

plage

3

Bout de Bois
Ref 4. 5.

D537

Acc 2.↓

↓ Nantes

D164

N

500m

see p.102
GR380

La Chevallerais

4 4

MAP 5

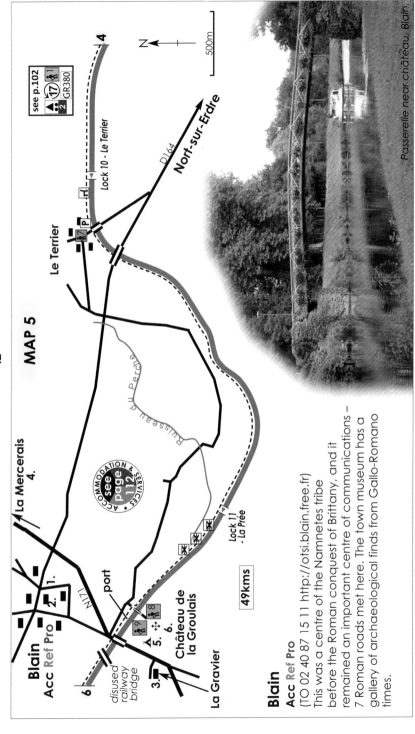

see p.102

GR380

La Mercerais
4.

Blain
Acc Ref Pro

port

disused
railway
bridge

Château de
la Groulais

La Gravier

Le Terrier

Lock 10 - Le Terrier

D164

Nort-sur-Erdre

Lock 11
- La Prée

49kms

N

500m

see page 112

ACCOMMODATION & SERVICES

Ruisseau du Perche

Blain
Acc Ref Pro

(TO 02 40 87 15 11 http://otsi.blain.free.fr)
This was a centre of the Namnetes tribe
before the Roman conquest of Brittany, and it
remained an important centre of communications –
7 Roman roads met here. The town museum has a
gallery of archaeological finds from Gallo-Romano
times.

Passerelle near château, Blain.

MAP 6

Blain
Acc
Ref Pro

5

D164

Lock 12 - Paudais

N
500m

53kms

7

see page 112 ACCOMMODATION & SERVICES

The impressive **Château de la Groulais**, on the south bank of the canal, dates back to the 12th century and the rule of Alain Fergent, Duke of Brittany. It was extended in the 14th century by Olivier de Clisson, before coming into the possession of the Rohans, one of medieval Brittany's greatest families. Henri de Rohan in the 17th century was a leader of Protestant reform, and after the Wars of Religion, the château at Blain was partly dismantled on the orders of Cardinal Richlieu. Further destruction followed in the Revolution, and in 1812 it was used as workshops for Spanish prisoners of war who were building the canal. The château then fell into disuse, until its restoration during the 20th century. The former *logis du roi* with its fine ceiling, is now a restaurant, and the château also hosts medieval re-enactments and events.
http://chateaudeblain.pagesperso-orange.fr
http://www.chateaudelagroulais.fr

Château de la Groulais

43

MAP 7

Forêt du Gâvre

This former ducal forest of 4500 acres lies just north of the canal here. Historically it has provided wood for numerous purposes from roof timbers to wine barrels, and sabots to ship-building.

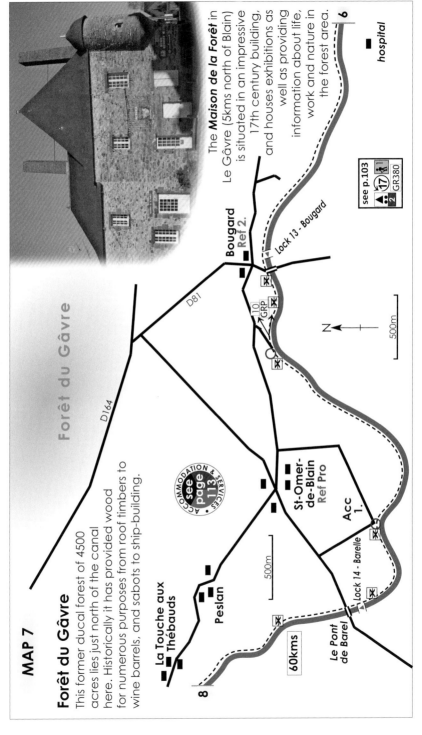

Forêt du Gâvre

The *Maison de la Forêt* in Le Gâvre (5kms north of Blain) is situated in an impressive 17th century building, and houses exhibitions as well as providing information about life, work and nature in the forest area.

hospital

D81

Bougard **Ref 2.**

Lock 13 - Bougard

GRP

10

D164

see p.103

GR380

N

500m

ACCOMMODATION & SERVICES • **see page 113**

St-Omer-de-Blain **Ref Pro**

Acc 1.

Lock 14 - Barelle

La Touche aux Thébauds

Peslan

500m

60kms

Le Pont de Barel

8

6

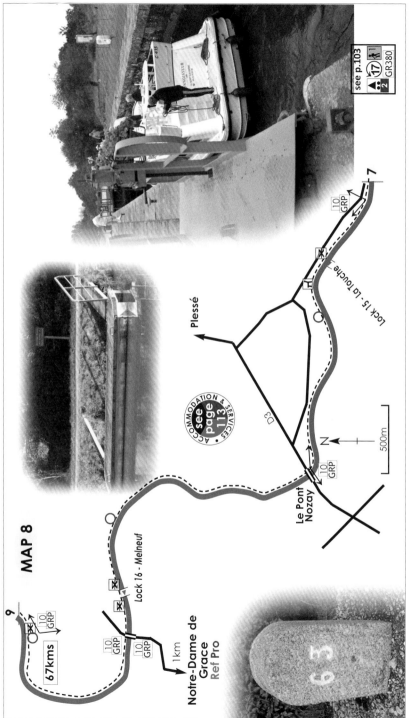

MAP 8

9

67kms

10 GRP

10 GRP

10 GRP

1 km

Lock 16 - Melneuf

Notre-Dame de
Grace
Ref Pro

SEE page 113

ACCOMMODATION & SERVICES

Plessé

D3

Le Pont
Nozay

10 GRP

N

500m

Lock 15 - La Touche

10 GRP

7

see p.103

17

2 GR380

6 3

MAP 9

Guenrouet Acc Ref Pro

The impressively situated church at Guenrouet is on a site of religious foundations dating back to the 11th century. An earlier structure faced the common revolutionary fate of serving as a stables, and its bells were melted down for coin. A new church was constructed in the 1890s, with a high, graceful bell tower finished in 1910.

As the Allies fought to liberate Brittany in 1944, the canal here marked the boundary between the Germans still firmly entrenched in St-Nazaire and the Americans, who shelled the villages in the vicinity over many months. On December 7 1944, the church tower at Guenrouet was destroyed. The church was eventually restored, and adorned by a series of stained-glass windows by Gabriel Loire from Chartres.

ACCOMMODATION & SERVICES
see page 113

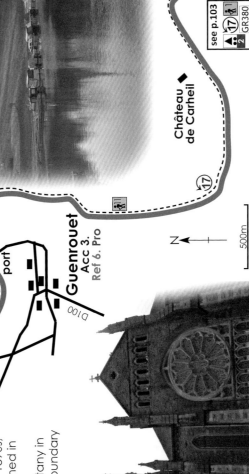

St-Clair

72kms

10

port

⚓ 4.

Guenrouet
Acc 3.
Ref 6. Pro

D100

N

500m

17

Château
de Carheil

see p.103
GR380

8

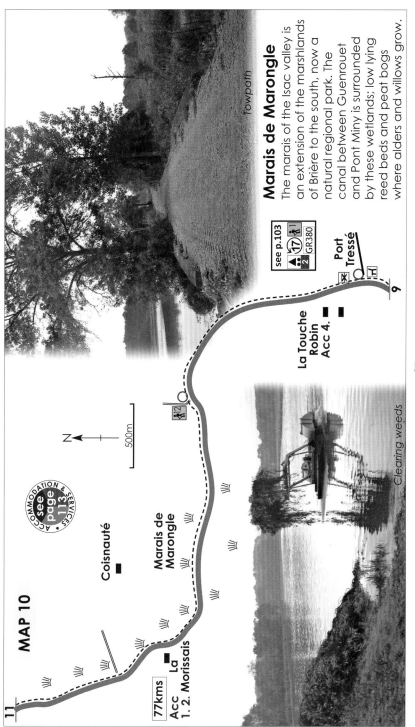

MAP 10

ACCOMMODATION & SERVICES
see page 113

N
500m

77kms
Acc
1. 2. Morissais

La

Coisnauté

Marais de Marongle

see p.103

GR380

La Touche
Robin
Acc 4.

Port
Tressé

9

11

Towpath

Marais de Marongle

The marais of the Isac valley is an extension of the marshlands of Brière to the south, now a natural regional park. The canal between Guenrouet and Pont Miny is surrounded by these wetlands; low lying reed beds and peat bogs where alders and willows grow.

Clearing weeds

48

Pont Miny Acc

The D773 crosses Pont Miny to reach the bourg of Fégréac, about 1km north of the canal. By the bridge is the *Maison du Canal* (see accommodation), with information and videos about the canal. On the opposite bank is a large 'aire de repos' with water and barbecue available.

see p.103

GR380

10

Nantes – Brest Canal

R. Isac

Acc 1.→

Freshwater crayfish strolling on the towpath

Maison du Canal
Pont Miny

MAP 11

Fégréac
Ref 4. Pro

D773

see page 113
ACCOMMODATION & SERVICES

500m

N

L'Hôtel
Ménant

10 GRP

Pont Miny Acc 2.
10 GRP Ref 3.

P

aire de repos

82kms

85

12

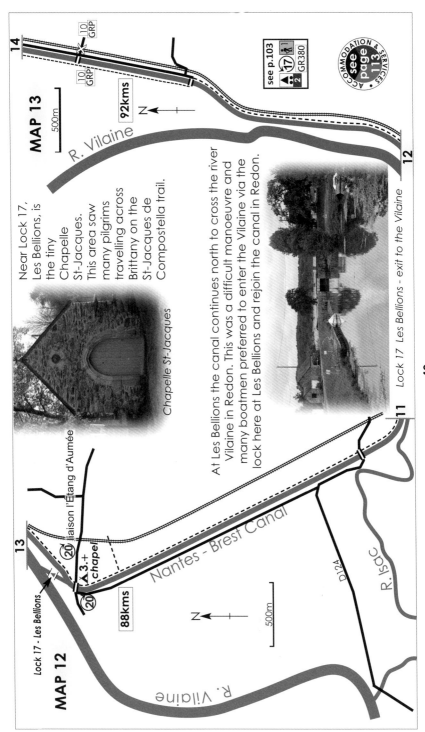

MAP 13

R. Vilaine

92kms

500m

see p.103
17 GR380

MAP 12

Lock 17 - Les Bellions

R. Vilaine

13

20 liaison l'Étang d'Aumée

20 ▲3.+ chapel

88kms

Nantes - Brest Canal

D124

R. Isac

Near Lock 17, Les Bellions, is the tiny Chapelle St-Jacques. This area saw many pilgrims travelling across Brittany on the St-Jacques de Compostella trail.

Chapelle St-Jacques

At Les Bellions the canal continues north to cross the river Vilaine in Redon. This was a difficult manoeuvre and many boatmen preferred to enter the Vilaine via the lock here at Les Bellions and rejoin the canal in Redon.

Lock 17 Les Bellions - exit to the Vilaine

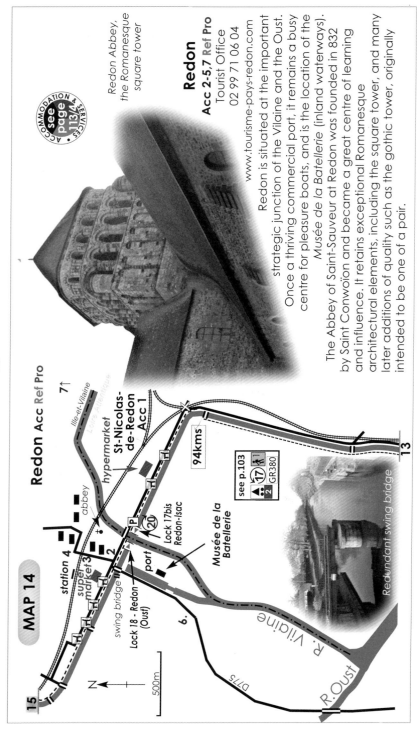

Redon Abbey,
the Romanesque
square tower

Redon

Acc 2-5,7 Ref Pro
Tourist Office
02 99 71 06 04
www.tourisme-pays-redon.com

Redon is situated at the important strategic junction of the Vilaine and the Oust. Once a thriving commercial port, it remains a busy centre for pleasure boats, and is the location of the *Musée de la Batellerie* (inland waterways).

The Abbey of Saint-Sauveur at Redon was founded in 832 by Saint Conwöion and became a great centre of learning and influence. It retains exceptional Romanesque architectural elements, including the square tower, and many later additions of quality such as the gothic tower, originally intended to be one of a pair.

see page 113/4

MAP 14

Redon Acc Ref Pro

Ille-et-Vilaine

Loire-Atlantique

7↑

hypermarket

St-Nicolas-de-Redon Acc 1

abbey

station 4

super market 3

swing bridge

Lock 18 - Redon (Oust)

Lock 17bis Redon-Isac

P 20

94kms

port

Musée de la Batellerie

see p.103
17
2 GR380

Redundant swing bridge

R. Vilaine

R. Oust

D775

13

6.

500m

N

Rivers Vilaine and Oust

8▲ Crossing the Vilaine at Redon, the Nantes-Brest canal passes from the department of Loire-Atlantique into Ille-et-Vilaine. The river Vilaine is navigable up to Rennes, where it is joined by the river Ille, here canalised and joined with the Rance to form a continuous navigable link between the Atlantic and the Channel at St-Malo. The Oust, rising in Côtes d'Armor near Quintin, flows into the Vilaine just south of Redon. The Nantes-Brest canal shadows the Oust to beyond Rohan, sometimes following its course, sometimes not, according to expediency.

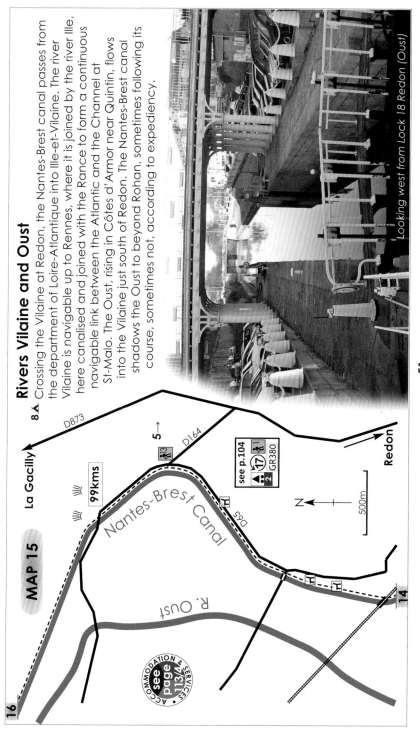

Looking west from Lock 18 Redon (Oust)

MAP 15

La Gacilly

D873

Nantes-Brest Canal

99kms

R. Oust

5 →

D164

D65

see p.104

GR380

Redon

500m

see page 113/4 ACCOMMODATION & SERVICES

16

14

51

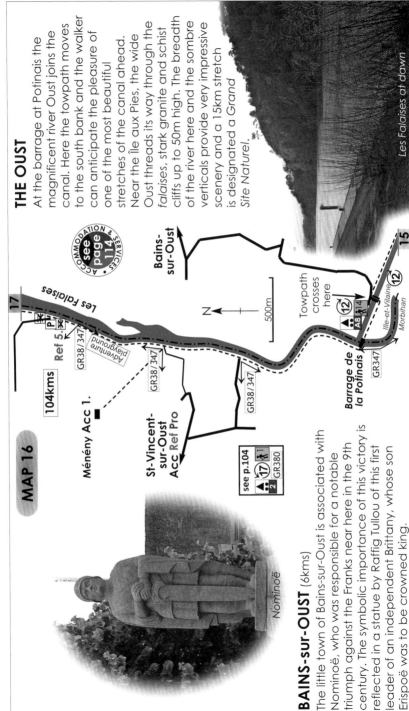

THE OUST

At the barrage at Potinais the magnificent river Oust joins the canal. Here the towpath moves to the south bank and the walker can anticipate the pleasure of one of the most beautiful stretches of the canal ahead. Near the île aux Pies, the wide Oust threads its way through the falaises, stark granite and schist cliffs up to 50m high. The breadth of the river here and the sombre verticals provide very impressive scenery and a 15km stretch is designated a Grand Site Naturel.

Les Falaises at dawn

MAP 16

see page 114

Bains-sur-Oust

Les Falaises

17

104kms

Ref 5.

GR38/347

Adventure playground

Ménény Acc 1.

St-Vincent-sur-Oust
Acc Ref Pro

GR38/347

GR38/347

see p.104
GR380

500m

Towpath crosses here

12

A8 1/4

Ille-et-Vilaine

Morbihan

GR347

Barrage de la Potinais

15

12

BAINS-sur-OUST (6kms)

The little town of Bains-sur-Oust is associated with Nominoë, who was responsible for a notable triumph against the Franks near here in the 9th century. The symbolic importance of this victory is reflected in a statue by Raffig Tullou of this first leader of an independent Brittany, whose son Erispoë was to be crowned king.

Nominoë

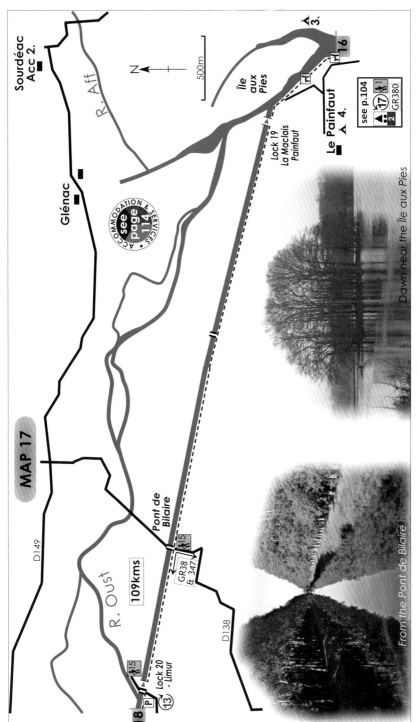

MAP 17

D149

R. Oust

109kms

Pont de Bilaire

🚶15

GR38 & 347

D138

18

P

🚶15

Lock 20 - Limur

⑬

Glénac

Sourdéac Acc 2.

R. Aff

ACCOMMODATION & SERVICES
see page 114

N

500m

île aux Pies

⚓ 3.

⌂ 16

⌂

Lock 19
La Maclais
Painfaut

Le Painfaut ⚓ 4.

see p.104

⚓2 ⑰ 🚶
GR380

From the Pont de Bilaire

Dawn near the île aux Pies

53

MAP 18

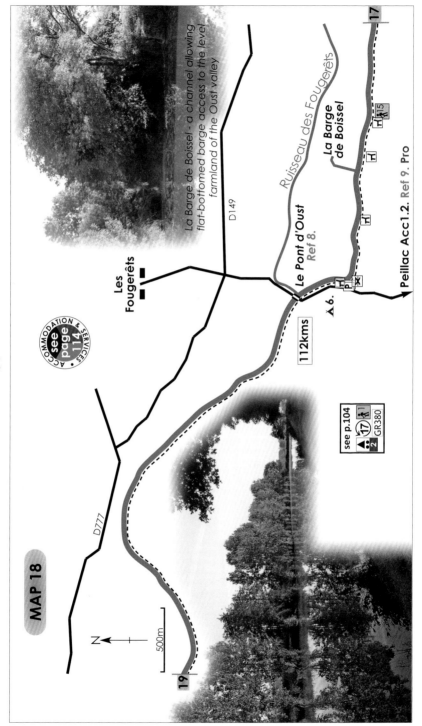

see page 114
ACCOMMODATION & SERVICES

Les Fougerêts

La Barge de Boissel - a channel allowing flat-bottomed barge access to the level farmland of the Oust valley

D149

Ruisseau des Fougerêts

La Barge de Boissel

Le Pont d'Oust
Ref 8.

▲ 6.

112kms

see p.104

17

2

GR380

D777

N

500m

19

17

15

Peillac Acc1.2. Ref 9. Pro

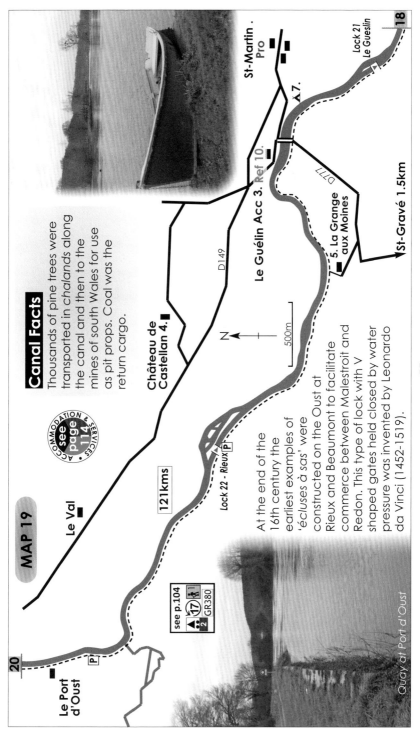

MAP 19

see p.104

17
2 GR380

121kms

Le Val ∎

**Le Port
d'Oust** ∎

Lock 22 - Rieux [P]

20

18

Canal Facts

Thousands of pine trees were transported in *chalands* along the canal and then to the mines of south Wales for use as pit props. Coal was the return cargo.

see page 114
• ACCOMMODATION & SERVICES •

**Château de
Castellan 4.** ∎

D149

N ↓

500m

**St-Martin .
Pro**

Le Guélin Acc 3. Ref 10.

Lock 21
Le Guelin

X 7.

D177

**5. La Grange
aux Moines** ∎

St-Gravé 1.5km →

At the end of the 16th century the earliest examples of 'écluses à sas' were constructed on the Oust at Rieux and Beaumont to facilitate commerce between Malestroit and Redon. This type of lock with V shaped gates held closed by water pressure was invented by Leonardo da Vinci (1452-1519).

Quay at Port d'Oust

55

MAP 20

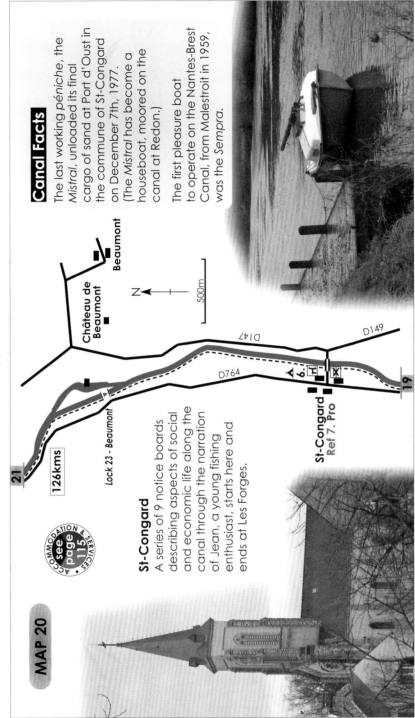

Canal Facts

The last working *péniche*, the *Mistral*, unloaded its final cargo of sand at Port d'Oust in the commune of St-Congard on December 7th, 1977. (The *Mistral* has become a houseboat, moored on the canal at Redon.)

The first pleasure boat to operate on the Nantes-Brest Canal, from Malestroit in 1959, was the *Sempra*.

Beaumont

Château de Beaumont

N ←
500m

D147

D149

D764

Lock 23 - Beaumont

21

126kms

see page 115
ACCOMMODATION & SERVICES

St-Congard
Ref 7. Pro

6.

19

St-Congard

A series of 9 notice boards describing aspects of social and economic life along the canal through the narration of Jean, a young fishing enthusiast, starts here and ends at Les Forges.

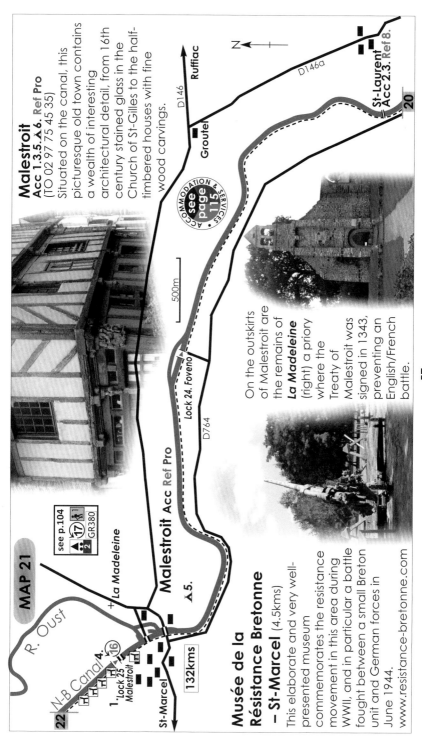

Malestroit

Acc 1.3.5.▲6. Ref Pro
(TO 02 97 75 45 35)

Situated on the canal, this picturesque old town contains a wealth of interesting architectural detail, from 16th century stained glass in the Church of St-Gilles to the half-timbered houses with fine wood carvings.

MAP 21

see p.104

GR380

R. Oust

N-B Canal

St-Marcel

Lock 25 Malestroit

▲5.

+ La Madeleine

Malestroit Acc Ref Pro

132kms

500m

Lock 24. Foveno

D764

D146

D146a

Ruffiac

Groutel

St-Laurent Acc 2.3. Ref 8.

22

20

16

17

N

see page 115

ACCOMMODATION & SERVICES

On the outskirts of Malestroit are the remains of *La Madeleine* (right) a priory where the Treaty of Malestroit was signed in 1343, preventing an English/French battle.

Musée de la Résistance Bretonne – St-Marcel (4.5kms)

This elaborate and very well-presented museum commemorates the resistance movement in this area during WWII, and in particular a battle fought between a small Breton unit and German forces in June 1944.

www.resistance-bretonne.com

57

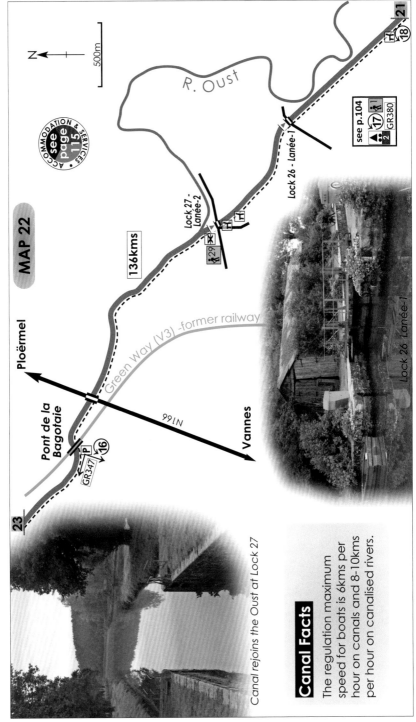

MAP 22

Ploërmel

Pont de la Bagotaie

GR347 P 16

23

Green way (V3) -former railway

N166

Vannes

136kms

Lock 27 - Lanée-2

29

Lock 26 - Lanée-1

R. Oust

ACCOMMODATION & SERVICES
see page 115

N
500m

see p.104
17 1
2 GR380

18
21

Lock 26 - Lanée-1

Canal rejoins the Oust at Lock 27

Canal Facts

The regulation maximum speed for boats is 6kms per hour on canals and 8-10kms per hour on canalised rivers.

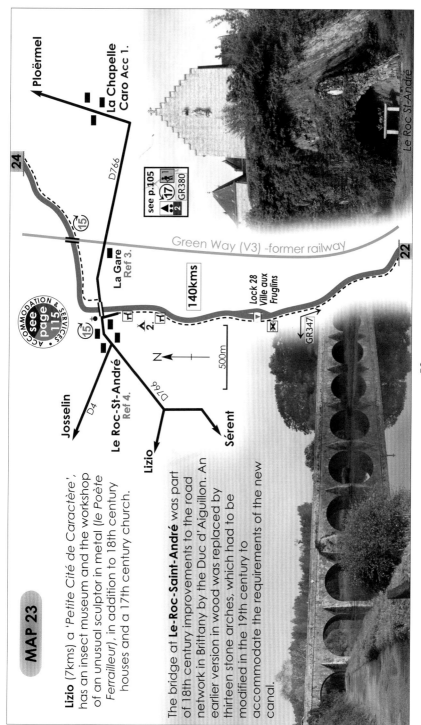

MAP 23

Lizio (7kms) a 'Petite Cité de Caractère', has an insect museum and the workshop of an unusual sculptor in metal (le Poète Ferrailleur), in addition to 18th century houses and a 17th century church.

The bridge at **Le-Roc-Saint-André** was part of 18th century improvements to the road network in Brittany by the Duc d'Aiguillon. An earlier version in wood was replaced by thirteen stone arches, which had to be modified in the 19th century to accommodate the requirements of the new canal.

Ploërmel

La Chapelle Caro Acc 1.

D766

Green Way (V3) -former railway

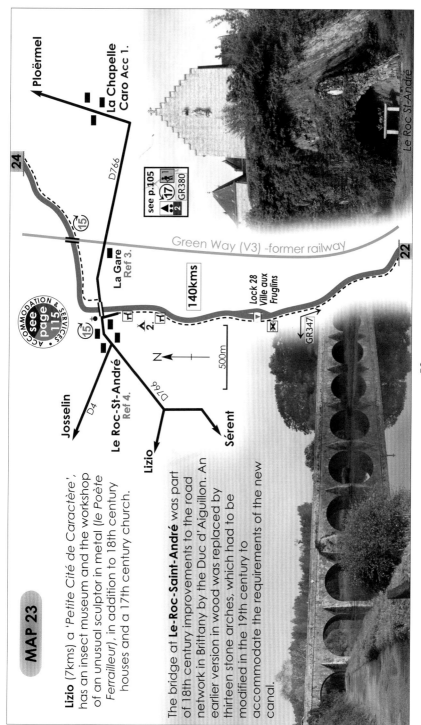
Le Roc St-André

see p.105
▲ 17 🍴
📷 2 GR380

La Gare Ref 3.

140kms

ACCOMMODATION & SERVICES
see page 115

15

15

🚻 🚻

⛺ 2.

N ⊢ 500m

Josselin

D4

Le Roc-St-André Ref 4.

D766

Lizio

Sérent

Lock 28 Ville aux Fruglins

🍴

GR347

24

22

59

MAP 24

WALK

There is a 8.4km circular walk (waymarked yellow) starting from the pike spawning pond (*frayère à brochets*)at Montertelot, passing by several wayside crosses, old villlages and a rock outcrop - *les rochers de St-Méen*.

(See 🚶)

Montertelot
Ref 4.5. Pro

P

Lock 29 Montertelot

800m to
La Chapelle-Caro
Ref Pro
Château du Crévy
Acc 3.

23

see p.105

17 GR380

2

500m

N

Green Way (V3) - former railway

R. Ninian

ACCOMMODATION & SERVICES
see page 115/4

Lock 30 - Blond

146kms

La Ville Nayl
Ref 6.

25

Quily
Ref 7. Pro

N166

D766

Montertelot

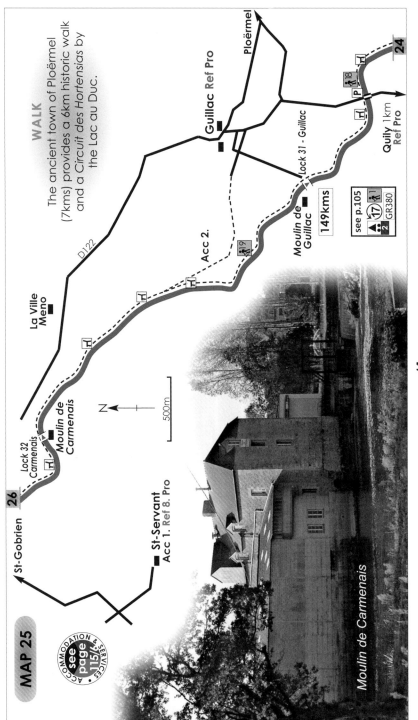

MAP 25

WALK

The ancient town of Ploërmel (7kms) provides a 6km historic walk and a *Circuit des Hortensias* by the Lac au Duc.

ACCOMMODATION & SERVICES
see **page 115/6**

500m

N

26 St-Gobrien

Lock 32 Carmenais

Moulin de Carmenais

St-Servant
Acc 1. Ref 8. Pro

La Ville Meno

D122

Acc 2.

Ploërmel

Guillac Ref Pro

Lock 31 - Guillac

Moulin de Guillac

149kms

Quily 1km
Ref Pro

24

P

see p.105
GR380

Moulin de Carmenais

61

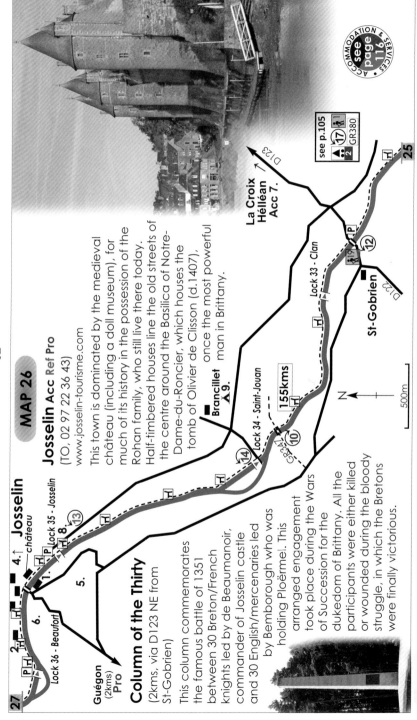

MAP 26

Josselin Acc Ref Pro

(TO, 02 97 22 36 43)
www.josselin-tourisme.com

This town is dominated by the medieval château (including a doll museum), for much of its history in the possession of the Rohan family, who still live there today. Half-timbered houses line the old streets of the centre around the Basilica of Notre-Dame-du-Roncier, which houses the tomb of Olivier de Clisson (d.1407), once the most powerful man in Brittany.

Guégon
(2kms)
Pro

Column of the Thirty

(2kms, via D123 NE from St-Gobrien)

This column commemorates the famous battle of 1351 between 30 Breton/French knights led by de Beaumanoir, commander of Josselin castle and 30 English/mercenaries led by Bemborough who was holding Ploërmel. This arranged engagement took place during the Wars of Succession for the dukedom of Brittany. All the participants were either killed or wounded during the bloody struggle, in which the Bretons were finally victorious.

Josselin
château

Lock 35 - Josselin
Lock 36 - Beaufort

Brancillet ▲9.

Lock 34 - Saint-Jouan

155kms

Lock 33 - Clan

St-Gobrien

La Croix
Hélléan
Acc 7.

see p.105
GR380

see page 116
ACCOMMODATION & SERVICES

N

500m

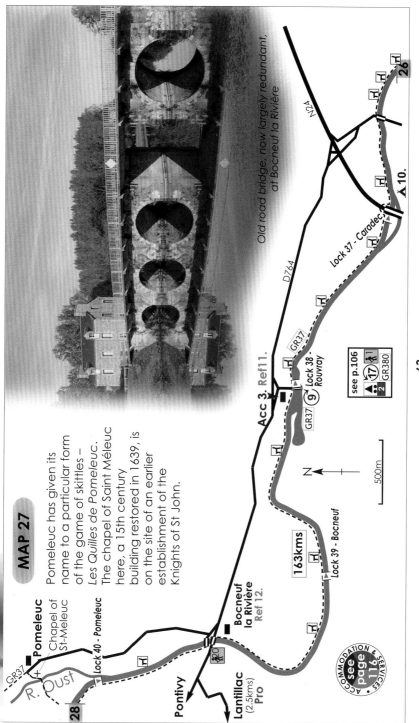

MAP 27

Pomeleuc has given its name to a particular form of the game of skittles – *Les Quilles de Pomeleuc*. The chapel of Saint Méleuc here, a 15th century building restored in 1639, is on the site of an earlier establishment of the Knights of St John.

Old road bridge, now largely redundant, at Bocneuf la Rivière

Pomeleuc
Chapel of St-Meleuc

GR37

R. Oust

28

Lock 40 - Pomeleuc

Pontivy

Bocneuf la Rivière
Ref 12.

Lantillac (2.5kms)
Pro

163kms

Lock 39 - Bocneuf

N

500m

Acc 3. Ref11.

9 Lock 38 - Rouvray

GR37

GR37

D764

Lock 37 - Caradec

N24

10.

26

see p.106

GR380

see page 116

ACCOMMODATION & SERVICES

63

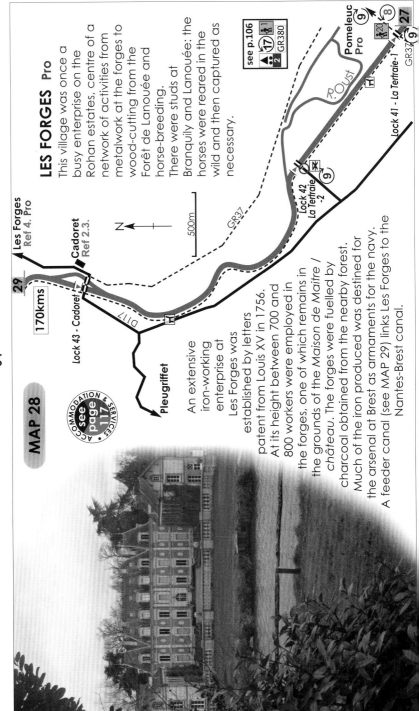

MAP 28

ACCOMMODATION & SERVICES · see page 117

LES FORGES Pro

This village was once a busy enterprise on the Rohan estates, centre of a network of activities from metalwork at the forges to wood-cutting from the Forêt de Lanouée and horse-breeding.

There were studs at Branquily and Lanouée: the horses were reared in the wild and then captured as necessary.

see p.106
GR380

Les Forges Ref 4. Pro

Cadoret Ref 2.3.

29

170kms

Lock 43 - Cadoret

D117

Pleugriffet

N 500m

GR37

Lock 42 La Terraie -2

9

R.OUST

Pomeleuc Pro 9

8

20

27

GR37 9

Lock 41 - La Terraie-1

GR37

An extensive iron-working enterprise at Les Forges was established by letters patent from Louis XV in 1756. At its height between 700 and 800 workers were employed in the forges, one of which remains in the grounds of the *Maison de Maître / château*. The forges were fuelled by charcoal obtained from the nearby forest. Much of the iron produced was destined for the arsenal at Brest as armaments for the navy. A feeder canal (see MAP 29) links Les Forges to the Nantes-Brest canal.

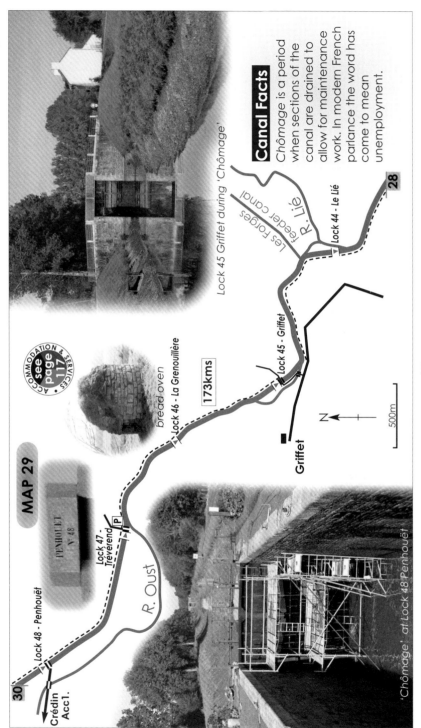

MAP 29

see page 117 ACCOMMODATION & SERVICES

Lock 48 - Penhouët

Crédin Accl.

Lock 47 - Trévérend

R. Oust

Lock 46 - La Grenouillère

bread oven

173kms

Lock 45 - Griffet

Griffet

N

500m

Lock 45 Griffet during 'Chômage'

Les Forges feeder canal

R. Lié

Lock 44 - Le Lié

Canal Facts

Chômage is a period when sections of the canal are drained to allow for maintenance work. In modern French parlance the word has come to mean unemployment.

'Chômage' at Lock 48 Penhouët

MAP 30

ACCOMMODATION & SERVICES • see page 117

Abbaye de Timadeuc

This 19th century Trappist foundation welcomes those seeking religious retreat. Attendance at some services is possible for visitors and there is a shop selling abbey products. A video explains the ethos of the community. In 1847 M.Cayot Délandre, during an exploration of Morbihan's history, visited the Abbey: 'the chant of 16 monks, full of richness and devout melody reached me. It was at once both harmonious and serious, with a melancholic charm which penetrated the soul and lifted one from the earth.'

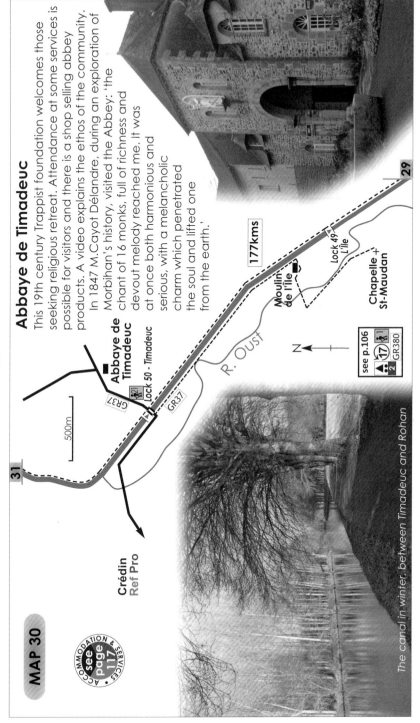

Crédin
Ref Pro

31

500m

GR37

Abbaye de
Timadeuc

Lock 50 - Timadeuc

GR37

R. Oust

177kms

Moulin
de l'île

Lock 49
L'île

Chapelle
St-Maudan

N

see p.106

GR380

29

The canal in winter, between Timadeuc and Rohan

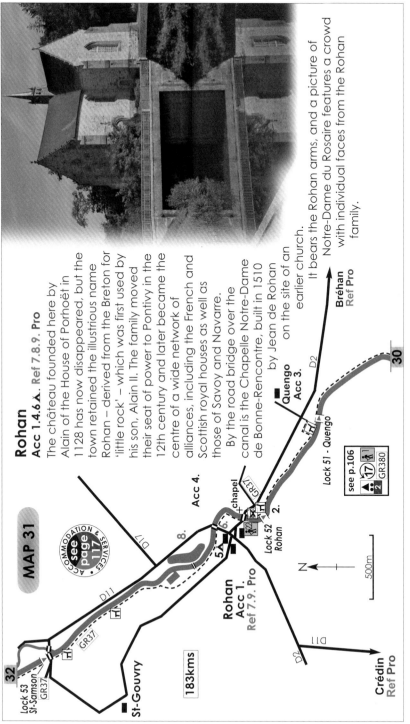

Rohan
Acc 1.4.6∆. Ref 7.8.9. Pro

The château founded here by Alain of the House of Porhoët in 1128 has now disappeared, but the town retained the illustrious name Rohan – derived from the Breton for 'little rock' – which was first used by his son, Alain II. The family moved their seat of power to Pontivy in the 12th century and later became the centre of a wide network of alliances, including the French and Scottish royal houses as well as those of Savoy and Navarre.

By the road bridge over the canal is the Chapelle Notre-Dame de Bonne-Rencontre, built in 1510 by Jean de Rohan on the site of an earlier church.

It bears the Rohan arms, and a picture of Notre-Dame du Rosaire features a crowd with individual faces from the Rohan family.

MAP 31

SEE PAGE 117 · ACCOMMODATION & SERVICES

183kms

32
Lock 53
St-Samson
GR37

D11

GR37

D17

8.

5. **6.**

chapel

Acc 4.

GR37

Lock 52
Rohan

Quengo
Acc 3.

D2

St-Gouvry

Rohan
Acc 1.
Ref 7.9. Pro

N

500m

D11

D2

Crédin
Ref Pro

see p.106

GR380

Lock 51 - Quengo

Quengo

Bréhan
Ref Pro

30

67

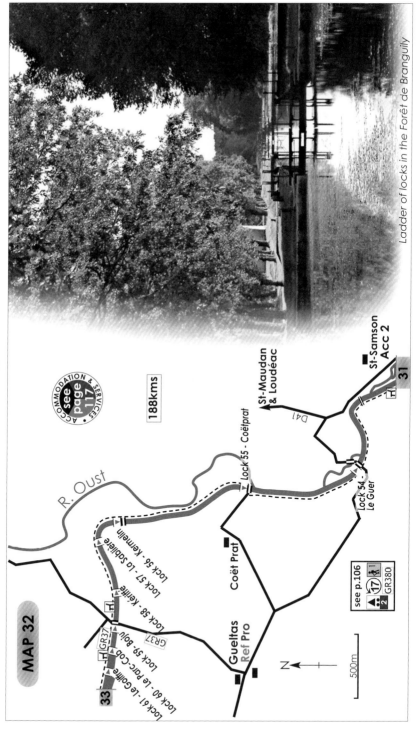

Ladder of locks in the Forêt de Branguily

68

MAP 32

R. Oust

188kms

see page 117 — ACCOMMODATION & SERVICES

31

33

St-Maudan & Loudéac

St-Samson Acc 2

D41

Lock 55 - Coëtprat

Lock 54 - Le Guer

Lock 56 - Kermelin

Lock 57 - La Sablière

Lock 58 - Keilffe

GR37

Lock 59 - Boju

Lock 60 - Le Parc-Cob

Lock 61 - Le Goffre

Coët Prat

Gueltas
Ref Pro

see p.106

GR380

N

500m

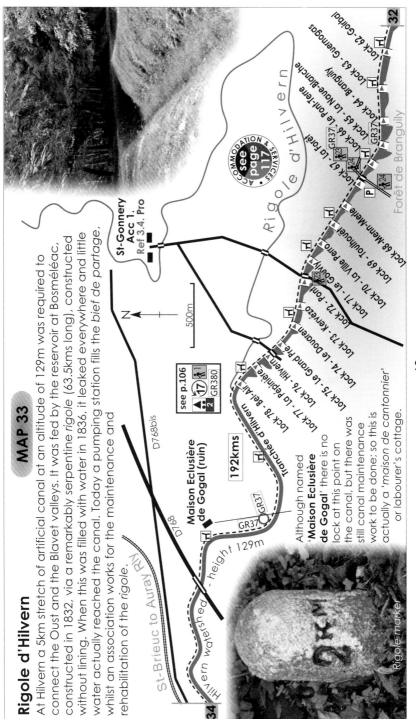

MAP 33

Rigole d'Hilvern

At Hilvern a 5km stretch of artificial canal at an altitude of 129m was required to connect the Oust and the Blavet valleys. It was fed by the reservoir at Bosméléac, constructed in 1832, via a remarkably serpentine *rigole* (63.5kms long), constructed without lining. When this was filled with water in 1836, it leaked everywhere and little water actually reached the canal. Today a pumping station fills the *bief de partage*, whilst an association works for the maintenance and rehabilitation of the *rigole*.

St-Gonnery
Acc 1.
Ref 3.4. Pro

R i g o l e d ' H i l v e r n

ACCOMODATION & SERVICES
page
117

St-Brieuc to Auray RN

D768

D768bis

N

500m

Hilvern watershed - height 129m

Tranchée d'Hilvern

Maison Eclusière de Gogal (ruin)

GR37

GR37

192kms

see p.106
17
2 GR380

Lock 78 - Bel-Air
Lock 77 - La Pépinière
Lock 76 - Hilvern
Lock 75 - Le Grand Pré
Lock 74 - Le Douaren
Lock 73 - Kervézo
Lock 72 - Pont
Lock 71 - La Ville Perro
Lock 70 - La Couly
Lock 69 - Toulhouët
Lock 68 - Mem-Méne

Forêt de Branguily

Lock 67 - La Forêt
Lock 66 - Le Pont-Terre
Lock 65 - La Noue-blanche
Lock 64 - Branguily
Lock 63 - Guémogas
Lock 62 - Golbal

GR37

P

GR37

32

34

Although named 'Maison Eclusière de Gogal' there is no lock at this point on the canal, but there was still canal maintenance work to be done; so this is actually a 'maison de cantonnier' or labourer's cottage.

Rigole-marker

69

70

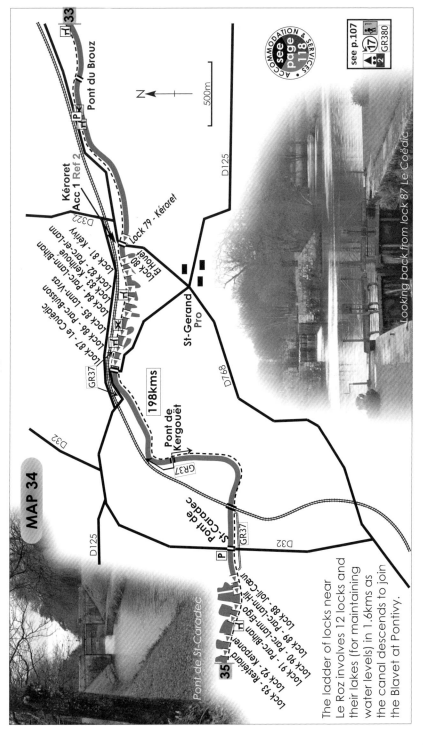

MAP 34

33

Pont du Brouz

P

Kéroret
Acc 1 Ref 2

D322

N

500m

Lock 79 - Kéroret

Lock 80 - Er Houël

Lock 81 - Kervry

Lock 82 - Parc-er-Lann

Lock 83 - Kerhouée

Lock 84 - Keilhoué-Bihan

Lock 85 - Lann-Vras

Lock 86 - Parc-Buisson

Lock 87 - Le Coëdic

GR37

198kms

Pont de Kergouët

GR37

St-Gerand
Pro

D768

D125

Pont de St-Caradec
St-Caradec

P

GR37

D32

D32

D125

Lock 88 - Joli-Cœur

Lock 89 - Parc-Lann-Hir

Lock 90 - Parc-Lann-Bigol

Lock 91 - Parc-Bihan

Lock 92 - Kerponer

Lock 93 - Resteland

35

Looking back from lock 87 Le Coëdic

see
page
118

see p.107

17

2

GR380

ACCOMMODATION & SERVICES

The ladder of locks near
Le Roz involves 12 locks and
their lakes (for maintaining
water levels) in 1.6kms as
the canal descends to join
the Blavet at Pontivy.

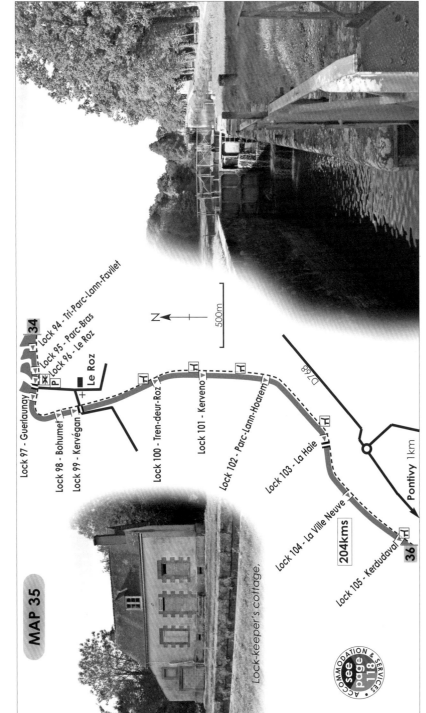

MAP 35

Lock 97 - Guerlaunay
Lock 94 - Tri-Parc-Lann-Favilet
Lock 95 - Parc-Bras
Lock 96 - Le Roz

34

Le Roz

Lock 98 - Bohumel
Lock 99 - Kervégan
Lock 100 - Tren-deur-Roz
Lock 101 - Kerveno
Lock 102 - Parc-Lann-Hoarem
Lock 103 - La Haie
Lock 104 - La Ville Neuve
Lock 105 - Kerdudaval

N

500m

D768

Pontivy 1km

204kms

36

Lock-keeper's cottage.

see page 118

ACCOMMODATION & SERVICES

71

MAP 36

see p.107

▲△17 🚶🏃
⚡2 GR380

37 **209kms**

35

Pontivy Acc 1– 8. Ref Pro TO 02 97 25 04 10 www.tourisme-pontivycommunaute.com

The Rohan château here, surrounded by streets of medieval houses, forms a contrast with the later Napoleonic development of this busy town. On several different occasions Pontivy took the name Napoleonville, according to the political climate of the time. It was intended by the imperial regime as a secure military and administrative centre in the volatile region of central Brittany where support for the Chouans (the Catholic anti-Republican movement) was strong.

Pontivy
Acc 1–7. Ref Pro

ACCOMMODATION & SERVICES
see page 118

Stival

R. Blavet

Lock 108 - La Cascade

D764

Mur-de-Bretagne

D767

GR37

GR37

Lock 106 - Kervert

Lock 107 - Le Ponteau

Lock 1 - Récollets
(Blavet Canal)

7.

4.

6. 2.

1.

Blavet

3.↓ ♿ 1.↓

5.↓

N

500m

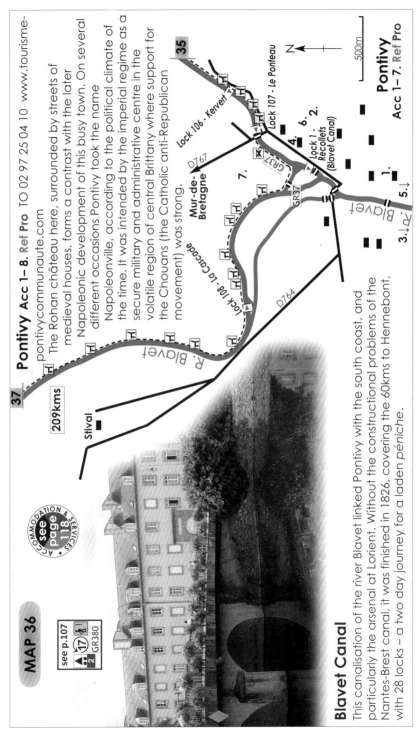

Blavet Canal

This canalisation of the river Blavet linked Pontivy with the south coast, and particularly the arsenal at Lorient. Without the constructional problems of the Nantes-Brest canal, it was finished in 1826, covering the 60kms to Hennebont, with 28 locks – a two day journey for a laden *péniche*.

Chapelle de Carmes

A signpost on the towpath points off towards the Chapelle Notre-Dame de Carmes. This essentially 15th century church has undergone various later phases of renewal. It's worth the 350m walk (if the chapel is open) to see the 18th century painted ceiling panels and those from the 15th century – showing scenes from the life of saint Catherine - discovered beneath them during restoration in the 1980s.

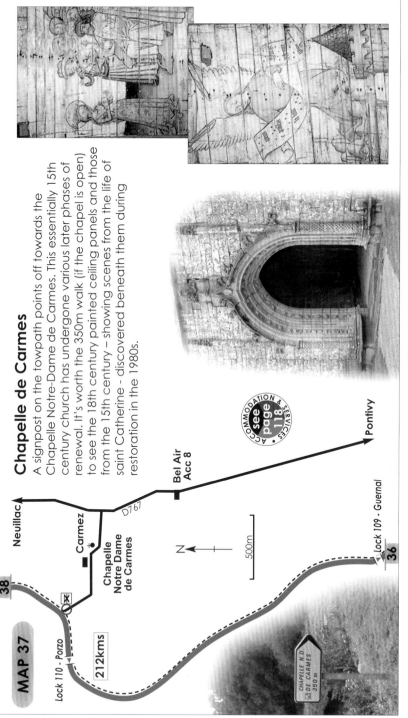

MAP 37

Neuillac

Carmez

Chapelle
Notre Dame
de Carmes

D767

Bel Air
Acc 8

Pontivy

Lock 110 - Porzo

212kms

Lock 109 - Guernal

38

36

500m

N

ACCOMMODATION & SERVICES
see page 118

CHAPELLE N.D
DE CARMES
350 m

MAP 38

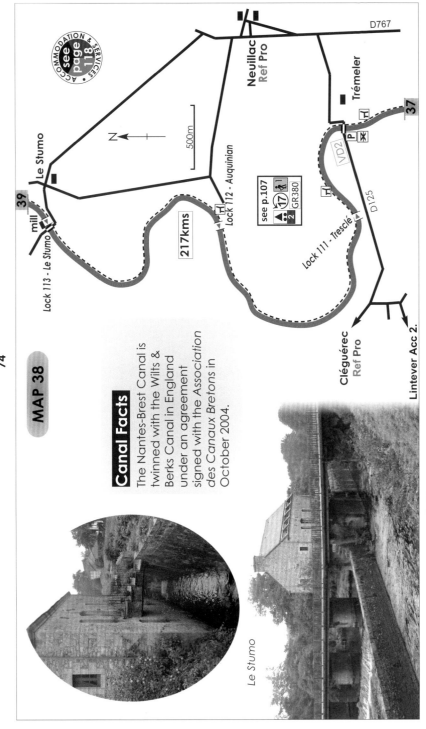

Canal Facts

The Nantes-Brest Canal is twinned with the Wilts & Berks Canal in England under an agreement signed with the Association des Canaux Bretons in October 2004.

Le Stumo

ACCOMMODATION & SERVICES • see page 118

D767

Neuillac
Ref Pro

Trémeler

Le Stumo

N

500m

mill

39

Lock 113 - Le Stumo

217kms

Lock 112 - Auquinian

see p.107
GR380
17
2

VD2

P

Lock 111 - Trescléo

D125

37

Cléguérec
Ref Pro

Lintever Acc 2.

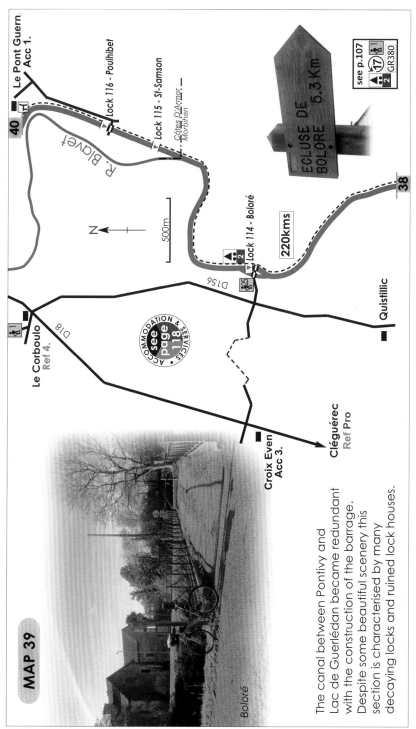

MAP 39

Le Pont Guern, Acc 1.

40

Lock 116 - Poulhibet

Lock 115 - St-Samson

R. Blavet

Côtes D'Armor
Morbihan

N ←

500m

38

Lock 114 - Boloré

220kms

ECLUSE DE
BOLORÉ 5.3 Km

see p.107

17 GR380
2

D156

Quistillic

Le Corboulo
Ref 4.

D18

**see
page 118**
ACCOMMODATION & SERVICES

Croix Even
Acc 3.

**Cléguérec
Ref Pro**

Boloré

The canal between Pontivy and
Lac de Guerlédan became redundant
with the construction of the barrage.
Despite some beautiful scenery this
section is characterised by many
decaying locks and ruined lock houses.

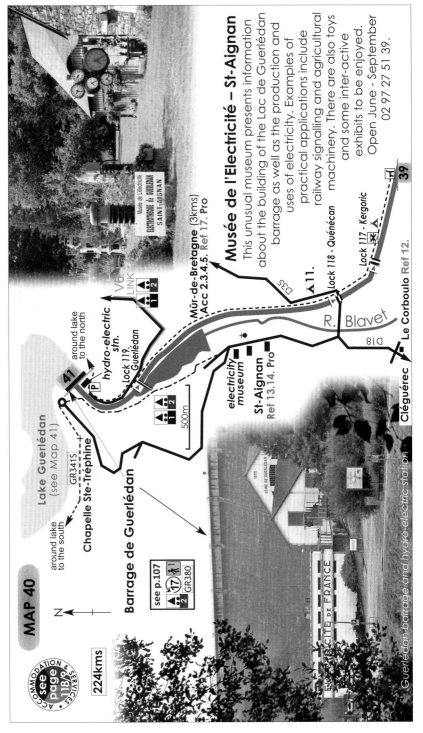

MAP 40

224kms

ACCOMMODATION & SERVICES see page 118/9

N

Lake Guerlédan
(see Map 41)

around lake
to the north

around lake
to the south

GR341S

Chapelle Ste-Tréphine

Barrage de Guerlédan

see p.107

GR380

41

P

hydro-electric
stn.

Lock 119, Guerlédan

500m

V6
LINK

Mûr-de-Bretagne (3kms)
Acc 2.3.4.5. **Ref 17. Pro**

electricity
museum

St-Aignan
Ref 13.14. Pro

R. Blavet

D35

▲11.

Lock 118 - Quénécan

Lock 117 - Kergoric

D18

Cléguérec

Le Corboulo Ref 12.

39

Musée de l'Electricité – St-Aignan

This unusual museum presents information about the building of the Lac de Guerlédan barrage as well as the production and uses of electricity. Examples of practical applications include railway signalling and agricultural machinery. There are also toys and some inter-active exhibits to be enjoyed.
Open June - September
02 97 27 51 39.

Guerlédan barrage and hydro-electric station

LAC DE GUERLEDAN (TO Mur-de-Bretagne 02 96 28 51 41)

Barrage de Guerlédan In 1923 permission was given for the creation of a lake and building of the barrage to generate electric power at Guerlédan. Twelve kilometres of the Blavet valley were flooded and the lake engulfed 400 hectares of woodland and houses including 18 locks from the former canal, together with the lock-keepers cottages. The original plan was to build a ladder of locks to keep passage along the canal open, but the cost was prohibitive and at a stroke the canal was cut in two. In September 1930 the barrage and its hydro-electric station were opened. It remains an impressive engineering feat at 206 metres long and 45m high, with 50,000,000 cubic metres of water filling the lake. Every ten years this was drained to allow inspection and maintenance – and a glimpse of the former canal's ruined houses and decaying locks.

Leisure

The lake is now a prime leisure resource, surrounded by walking and cycling trails. The VTT station at *Le Rond Point* has bike hire and information about 300kms of marked circuits in the vicinity of the lake.

There are also **centres nautiques** at *Beau Rivage*, the *Anse de Sordan*, and *Le Rond-Point du Lac*. At these points you can hire canoes and pedal boats, and swimming beaches provide easy access to the water. Cruises (including lunch/dinner on board) by the *Vedettes de Guerlédan* are available from *Beau Rivage*.

Walking and cycling around the lake

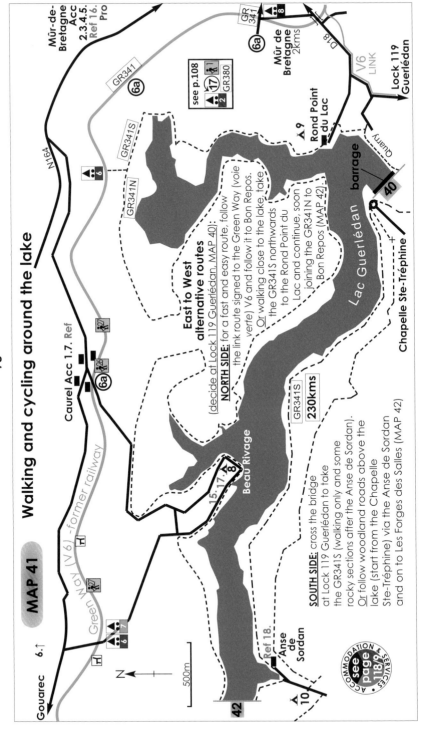

MAP 41

Gouarec 6.↑

Green Way (V6) - former railway

N164

Caurel Acc 1.7. Ref

Mûr-de-Bretagne Acc 2.3.4.5. Ref 16. Pro

GR341

GR341

6a

GR341S

GR341N

6a

see p.108
GR380

Mûr de Bretagne 2kms

V6 LINK

D18

Lock 119 Guerlédan

Rond Point du Lac

△ 9

GR341S

230kms

Beau Rivage

Lac Guerlédan

barrage

40

Chapelle Ste-Tréphine

Quarry

East to West alternative routes
(decide at Lock 119 Guerlédan, MAP 40):

NORTH SIDE: for a fast and easy route, follow the link route signed to the Green Way (voie verte) V6 and follow it to Bon Repos. Or walking close to the lake, take the GR341S northwards to the Rond Point du Lac and continue, soon joining the GR341N to Bon Repos (MAP 42).

SOUTH SIDE: cross the bridge at Lock 119 Guerlédan to take the GR341S (walking only and some rocky sections after the Anse de Sordan). Or follow woodland roads above the lake (start from the Chapelle Ste-Tréphine) via the Anse de Sordan and on to Les Forges des Salles (MAP 42)

Ref 18.

Anse de Sordan

△ 10

42

N

500m

ACCOMMODATION & SERVICES
see page 118/9

15.17
8

Conomor and the Chapelle Ste-Tréphine

Conomor, an historical figure of 6th century Breton history, has also acquired a legendary image as a Breton bluebeard. He decapitated his young pregnant wife Tréphine, to avoid fulfillment of the prophecy that his

son would kill him. Saint Gildas intervened to bring Tréphine back to life, but years later Conomor did succeed in killing Trémeur, the young boy she bore. His ruthlessness (and aggressive expansionism as a powerful ruler) led to excommunication and many bloody conflicts with his rivals.

A 700m detour from the carpark by the barrage will lead to the chapel of Ste-Tréphine (and an easier path above the forest, if required).

A little way along the lakeside route GR341S, the outcrop of Kastell Finians, once a stronghold of

The GR341S

Conomor, rises above the lake. It provided a strategic base for defending important mineral resources, such as the gold of the Blavet river valley, and lead-silver mines of Poullaouen in his home territory of Poher.

Chapelle de Ste-Tréphine

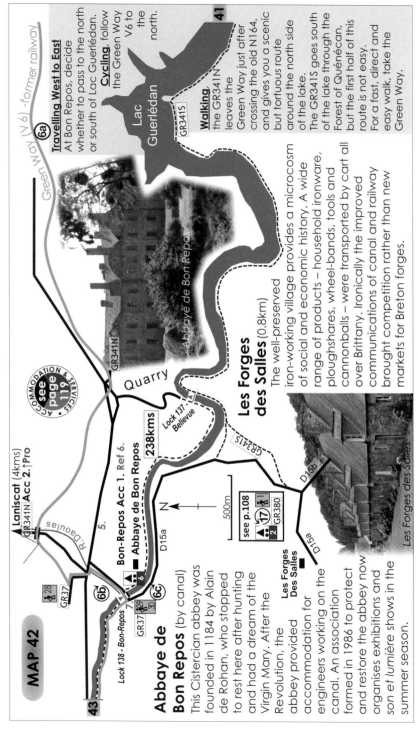

MAP 42

Green Way (V6) - former railway

Travelling West to East
At Bon Repos, decide whether to pass to the north or south of Lac Guerlédan. **Cycling**: follow the Green Way V6 to the north.

Walking: the GR341N leaves the Green Way just after crossing the old N164, and gives you a scenic but tortuous route around the north side of the lake. The GR341S goes south of the lake through the Forest of Quénécan, but the first half of this route is not easy. For a fast, direct and easy walk, take the Green Way.

41

Lac Guerlédan

GR341S

GR341N

Abbaye de Bon Repos

ACCOMMODATION & SERVICES
see page 119

Quarry

Les Forges des Salles (0.8km)
The well-preserved iron-working village provides a microcosm of social and economic history. A wide range of products – household ironware, ploughshares, wheel-bands, tools and cannonballs – were transported by cart all over Brittany. Ironically the improved communications of canal and railway brought competition rather than new markets for Breton forges.

Les Forges des Salles

Lock 137 - Bellevue

238kms

GR341S

D15b

see p.108
500m
GR380
N

Les Forges Des Salles

D15a

6c

Laniscat (4kms)
GR341N Acc 2.↑Pro

R.Daoulas
GR37

28
GR37

43

6b
GR37
30

Lock 138 - Bon-Repos

Bon-Repos Acc 1. Ref 6.
■ Abbaye de Bon Repos

5.

D15a

7.

Abbaye de Bon Repos (by canal)
This Cistercian abbey was founded in 1184 by Alain de Rohan, who stopped to rest here after hunting and had a dream of the Virgin Mary. After the Revolution, the abbey provided accommodation for engineers working on the canal. An association formed in 1986 to protect and restore the abbey now organises exhibitions and son et lumière shows in the summer season.

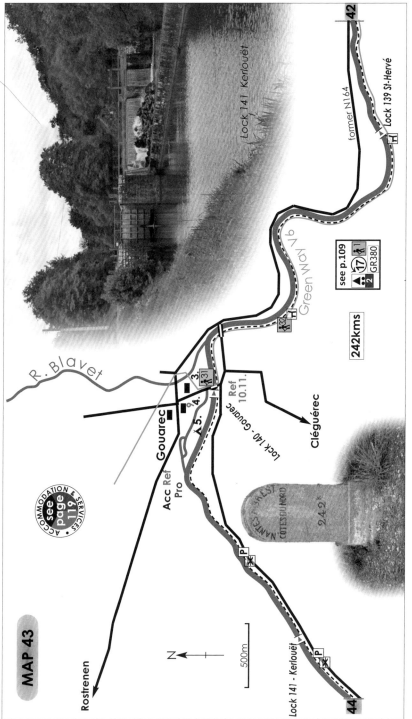

MAP 43

Rostrenen

N ←

500m

R. Blavet

Gouarec

Acc Ref Pro

SEE page 119 · ACCOMMODATION & SERVICES ·

3.
🚶3
○ 4.
⛺ 5.

🚶32 H

Lock 140 - Gouarec

Ref 10.11.

Cléguérec

NANTES·BREST
CÔTESDUNORD
24.2k

Green Way V6

see p.109
🚶17
⛺2 GR380

242kms

Lock 141 Kerlouët

former N164

Lock 139 St-Hervé
H

42

Lock 141 - Kerlouët

🅿
🍴

🅿
🍴

44

81

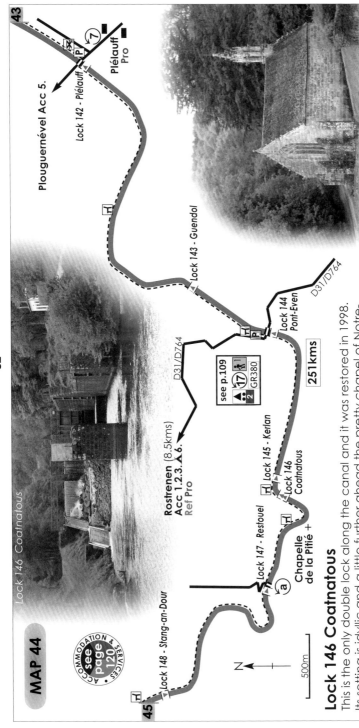

MAP 44

SEE page 120 ACCOMMODATION & SERVICES

N

500m

Lock 146 Coatnatous

La Chapelle de la Pitié

43

Plouguernével Acc 5.

Lock 142 - Plélauff

Plélauff
Pro

7

P

Lock 143 - Guendol

Lock 144
Pont-Even

D31/D764

251kms

see p.109
GR380

Rostrenen (8.5kms)
Acc 1.2.3. 6.
Ref Pro

D31/D764

Lock 145 - Kerlan

Lock 146
Coatnatous

Lock 147 - Restouel

Chapelle
de la Pitié +

a

Lock 148 - Stang-an-Dour

45

Lock 146 Coatnatous

This is the only double lock along the canal and it was restored in 1998. Its setting is idyllic and a little further ahead the pretty chapel of Notre-Dame de la Pitié, together with its *fontaine*, comes into view across the water. There are also traces of a Roman bridge nearby and a prehistoric camp on the hill opposite the lock.

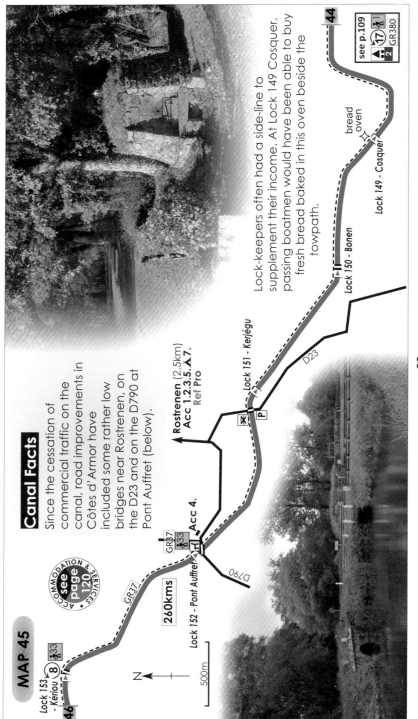

MAP 45

Canal Facts

Since the cessation of commercial traffic on the canal, road improvements in Côtes d'Armor have included some rather low bridges near Rostrenen, on the D23 and on the D790 at Pont Auffret (below).

Lock-keepers often had a side-line to supplement their income. At Lock 149 Cosquer, passing boatmen would have been able to buy fresh bread baked in this oven beside the towpath.

ACCOMMODATION & SERVICES · **see page 120**

Rostrenen (2.5km) Acc 1.2.3.5.▲7. Ref Pro

Lock 153 - Kériou ⑧ 🛏33

46

500m
N

GR37

260kms

GR37 🛏33
Acc 4.
Lock 152 - Pont Auffret

D790

P
🍴

Lock 151 - Keriégu

D23

Lock 150 - Bonen

bread oven

Lock 149 - Cosquer

see p.109
🏃17 GR380
▲2

44

83

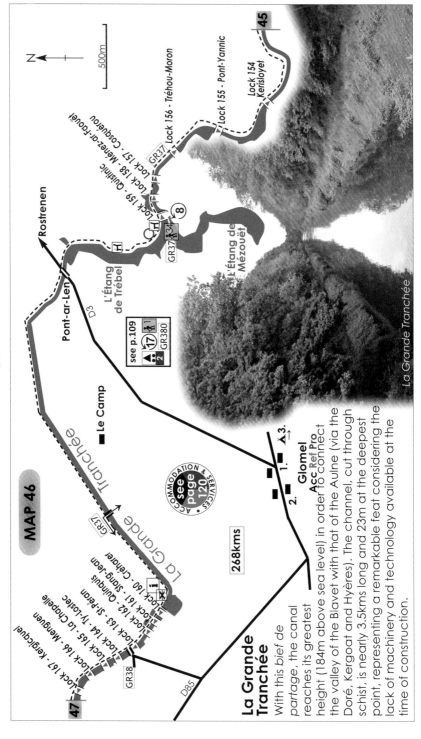

MAP 46

La Grande Tranchée

268kms

Rostrenen

Pont-ar-Len

D3

L'Étang de Trébel

Le Camp

La Grande Tranchée

GR37

Lock 160 - Créhalet
Lock 161 - Stang-Jean
Lock 162 - Quinquis
Lock 163 - St-Péran
Lock 164 - Ty-Lostec
Lock 165 - La Chapelle
Lock 166 - Menguen
Lock 167 - Kergiquel

GR38

D85

47

ACCOMMODATION & SERVICES
see page 120

see p.109
17
GR380
2

GR37

8
GR37

Lock 159 - Gustinic
Lock 158 - Menez-ar-Faouet
Lock 157 - Coszuélou
Lock 156 - Tréhou-Moron
GR37
Lock 155 - Pont-Yannic
Lock 154 Kerisloyet

45

L'Étang de Mézouët

500m
N

Glomel
Acc Ref Pro
1.
2.
3.

La Grande Tranchée

With this bief de *partage*, the canal reaches its greatest height (184m above sea level) in order to connect the valley of the Blavet with that of the Aulne (via the Doré, Kergoat and Hyères). The channel, cut through schist, is nearly 3.5kms long and 23m at the deepest point, representing a remarkable feat considering the lack of machinery and technology available at the time of construction.

La Grande Tranchée

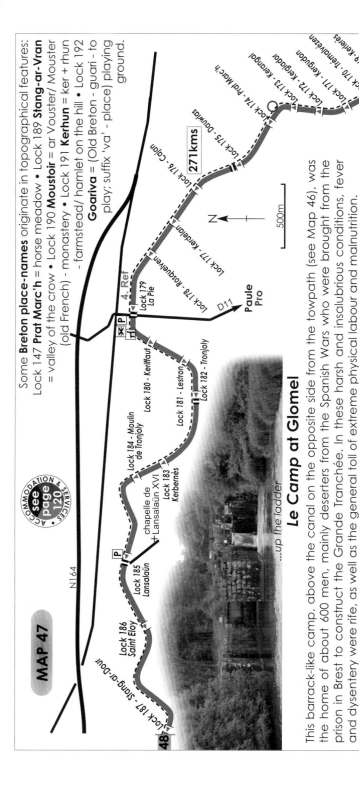

MAP 47

Some **Breton place-names** originate in topographical features: Lock 147 **Prat Marc'h** = horse meadow • Lock 189 **Stang-ar-Vran** = valley of the crow • Lock 190 **Moustoir** = ar Vouster/ Mouster (old French) - monastery • Lock 191 **Kerhun** = ker + rhun - farmstead/ hamlet on the hill • Lock 192 **Goariva** = (Old Breton - guari - to play; suffix 'va' - place) playing ground.

N164

P

P

Lock 187 - Stang-ar-Dour

Lock 186 Saint Eloy

Lock 185 Lansalaün

chapelle de + Lansalaün XVI

Lock 184 - Moulin de Tronjoly

Lock 183 Kerbernès

Lock 182 - Tronjoly

Lock 181 - Lestron

Lock 180 - Keriffaut

...up the ladder

Lock 179 La Pie

Lock 178 - Rosquelfen

4 Ref

Lock 177 - Kerledan

271kms

N

500m

Lock 176 - Cajan

Lock 175 - Douvigas

Lock 174 - Prat Marc'h

Lock 173 - Kergod   Lock 172 - Kergadou

Lock 171 - Kergudon

Lock 170 - Tremalvézen

Lock 189 - Kerletés

Lock 168 - Kermarerhquer

46

48

D11

Paule Pro

SEE page 120 ACCOMMODATION & SERVICES

85

Le Camp at Glomel

This barrack-like camp, above the canal on the opposite side from the towpath (see Map 46), was the home of about 600 men, mainly deserters from the Spanish Wars who were brought from the prison in Brest to construct the Grande Tranchée. In these harsh and insalubrious conditions, fever and dysentery were rife, as well as the general toll of extreme physical labour and malnutrition. In the aftermath of the 1830 revolution in Paris, many prisoners broke out of the camp, some to roam the countryside around Glomel and Rostrenen, but about 200 others to make for the military and administrative centre of Pontivy to secure confirmation of their newly acclaimed right to liberty. The camp was finally closed in 1832 and much of it destroyed by fire several years later.

MAP 48

Carhaix
3.5kms

Carhaix Acc 1.2.5.6. Ref Pro

Carhaix (Vorgium) was an important settlement in Roman times, having earlier been the centre of the Osismes tribe. Ever since it has been the centre of a communications network – road and rail - for western Brittany. Traces of the Roman aqueduct, a mainly subterranean canal, which brought water to the town from 27kms away can still be seen, and a programme of archaeological excavation uncovering Roman streets, shops and villas continues annually. The Tourist Office (02 98 93 04 42) is housed in the 16th century Maison du Seneschal.

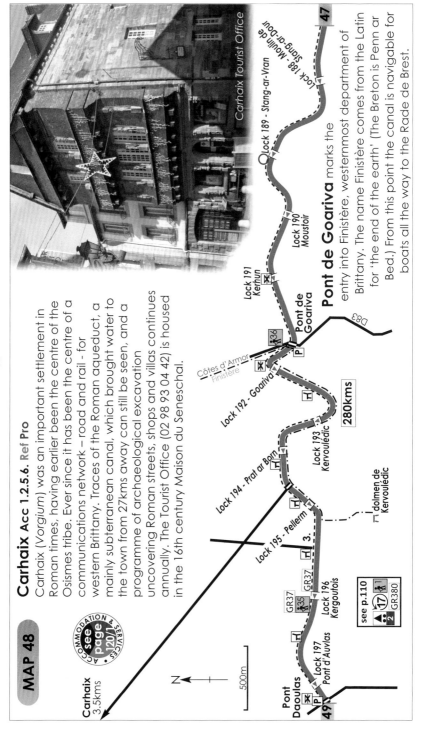

Carhaix Tourist Office

Lock 189 - Stang-ar-Vran

Lock 188 - Moulin de
Stang-ar-Dour

47

Lock 190
Moustoir

Lock 191
Kerhun

Pont de
Goariva

Pont de Goariva marks the entry into Finistère, westernmost department of Brittany. The name Finistère comes from the Latin for 'the end of the earth'. (The Breton is Penn ar Bed.) From this point the canal is navigable for boats all the way to the Rade de Brest.

D83

Côtes d'Armor
Finistère

Lock 192 - Goariva

280kms

Lock 193
Kervouléic

Lock 194 - Prat ar Born

dolmen de
Kervouléic

Lock 195 - Pellerm   3.

GR37
GR37

Lock 196
Kergoutois

see p.110

17
2
GR380

Lock 197
Pont d'Auvlas

Pont
Daoulas

49

500m

N

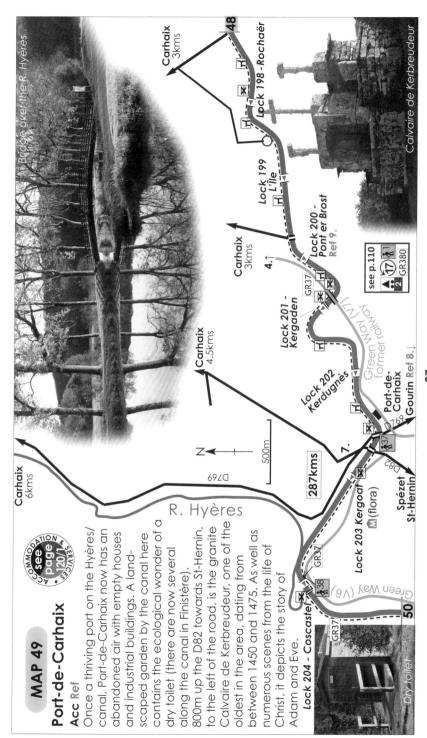

MAP 49

Port-de-Carhaix

Acc Ref

Once a thriving port on the Hyères/canal, Port-de-Carhaix now has an abandoned air with empty houses and industrial buildings. A land-scaped garden by the canal here contains the ecological wonder of a dry toilet (there are now several along the canal in Finistère).

800m up the D82 towards St-Hernin, to the left of the road, is the granite Calvaire de Kerbreudeur, one of the oldest in the area, dating from between 1450 and 1475. As well as numerous scenes from the life of Christ, it depicts the story of Adam and Eve.

ACCOMMODATION & SERVICES
see page 120/1

Bridge over the R. Hyères

Calvaire de Kerbreudeur

Carhaix 6kms

D769

R. Hyères

Carhaix 4.5kms

N

500m

287kms

7.

Carhaix 3kms

4.↑

Lock 202 - Kerdugnès

Lock 201 - Kergaden

GR37

Green former railway

Carhaix 3kms

Gourin Way (V7)

Port-de-Carhaix

Gourin Ref 8.↓

D769

Lock 200 - Pont er Brost Ref 9.

Lock 199 L'île

Lock 198 - Rochaër

Carhaix 3kms

48

see p.110

17

2 GR380

Spézet St-Hernin

D82

Lock 203 Kergoat

🌼 (flora)

GR37

Green Way (V6)

Lock 204 - Coscastel

GR37

38

50

Dry toilet

87

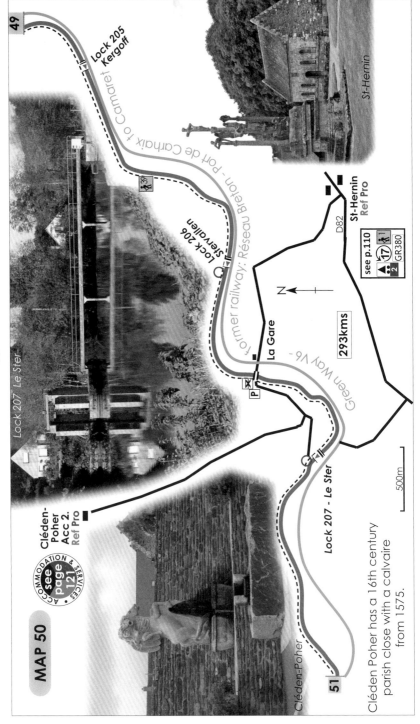

MAP 50

ACCOMMODATION & SERVICES
see page 121

Cléden-
Poher
Acc 2.
Ref Pro

Lock 207 - Le Ster

Lock 207 - Le Ster

Lock 206
Servallen

Lock 205
Kergoff

former railway: Réseau Breton - Port de Carhaix to Camaret

La Gare

P

- Green Way V6 -

293kms

N

St-Hernin
Ref Pro

D82

see p.110

17 ▲ 2 GR380

500m

St-Hernin

Cléden-Poher

49

51

Cléden Poher has a 16th century parish close with a calvaire from 1575.

MAP 51

Maison du Canal
at Ecluse 209 Pont Triffen.

This information point is open from July to September, with information about the history and construction of the canal and reference books for consultation. It is run by SMATAH, a group which promotes the heritage and environment of the Aulne and the Hyères, and develops educational projects. (Their base is at Châteauneuf-du-Faou 02 98 73 40 31)

■ Landelau Acc 3.4. Pro

R. Hyères

Lock 208
Lesnevé

50

(V6)

Lock 209
Pont-Triffen

Ref 7.
Pont Triffen

Pont Triffen

Here is a conglomeration of communications: the old railway line from Carhaix to Camaret, overhead the N164 motorway, whilst beneath the mighty river Aulne (Ster Aon in Breton) swoops down from the north and its humble origins near the Forêt de Beffou to take over the business of the canal from the Hyères.

Spézet
Acc 1.2.
Ref Pro

R. Aulne

▲5.

Lock 210 - **Pénity**

300kms

N164

see page 121

ACCOMMODATION & SERVICES

Lock 211
Rosgohuen

see p.110

17
GR380

N

Lock 212
Méros
(Kerganéver)

R. Aulne

500m

52

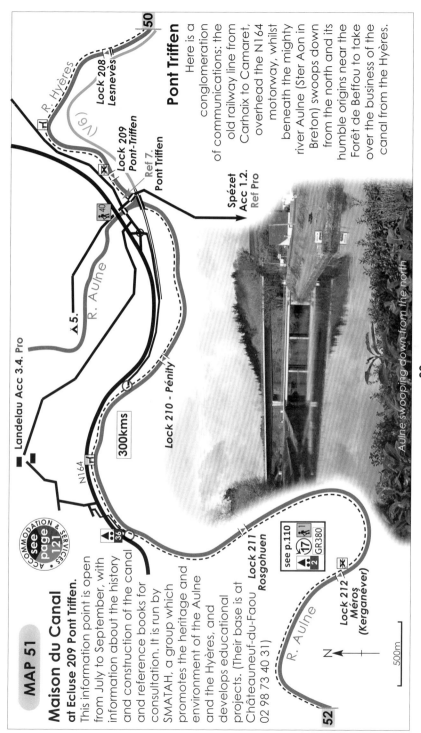

Aulne swooping down from the north

89

MAP 52

Château de Trévarez

(1.5kms from Ecluse 217 Boudrac'h)

Called the 'château rose', this late 19th century construction was badly damaged by English bombs in WWII when it was occupied by the Germans. The grounds are justly famous for an exceptional display of azaleas, rhododendrons and camellias. Exhibitions are held in the old stables area where there are also a shop and café. www.cdp29.fr

ACCOMMODATION & SERVICES see page 121/2

Châteauneuf-du-Faou (on the canal) TO - 02 98 81 83 90

Acc 1.2.6. Ref 11. Pro

This charming little town (a steep walk up from the canal) with its flowery squares has a good range of shops and places to eat. The Chapel of Notre Dame des Portes, in its dramatic location high above the canal, is a 19th century church on the site of the original château. The small building beside it, built from stones from the château, retains an impressive 15th doorway. In the town centre, the Church of St Julien has a chapel decorated with paintings by Paul Sérusier, one of the Pont Aven group of artists, who spent the later part of his life here.

Boats can be hired from Aulne Loisirs, on the canal beyond the road bridge.

Paul Sérusier painting

Acc 3.

Lock 213 Rosily

308kms

Lock 214 Lanmeur

Pont du Stang

Spézet

500m

D117

Châteauneuf -du-Faou

Pont du Roy in high water

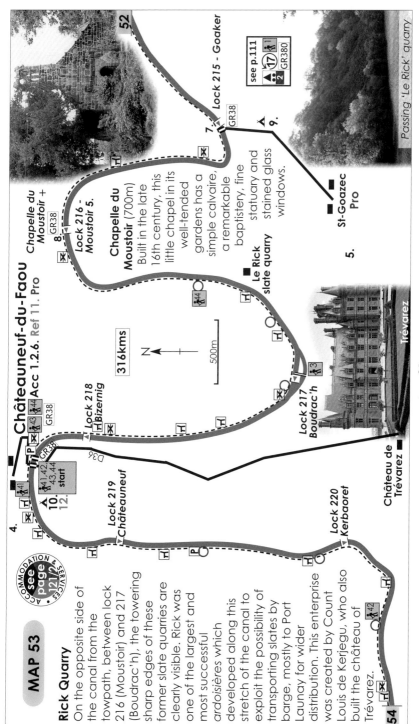

MAP 53

Rick Quarry

On the opposite side of the canal from the towpath, between lock 216 (Moustoir) and 217 (Boudrac'h), the towering sharp edges of these former slate quarries are clearly visible. Rick was one of the largest and most successful ardoisières which developed along this stretch of the canal to exploit the possibility of transporting slates by barge, mostly to Port Launay for wider distribution. This enterprise was created by Count Louis de Kerjegu, who also built the château of Trévarez.

ACCOMMODATION & SERVICES
see page 121/2/4

Châteauneuf-du-Faou
Acc 1.2.6. Ref 11. Pro

Chapelle du Moustoir +

Lock 215 - Goaker

see p.111
GR380

Lock 216 - Moustoir 5.

Chapelle du Moustoir (700m)
Built in the late 16th century, this little chapel in its well-tended gardens has a simple calvaire, a remarkable baptistery, fine statuary and stained glass windows.

St-Goazec Pro

Le Rick slate quarry

Lock 218 Bizernig
GR38

316kms

N
500m

Lock 217 Boudrac'h

Lock 219 Châteauneuf
GR38
D36
start

Lock 220 Kerbaoret

Château de Trévarez

Trévarez

Passing 'Le Rick' quarry

91

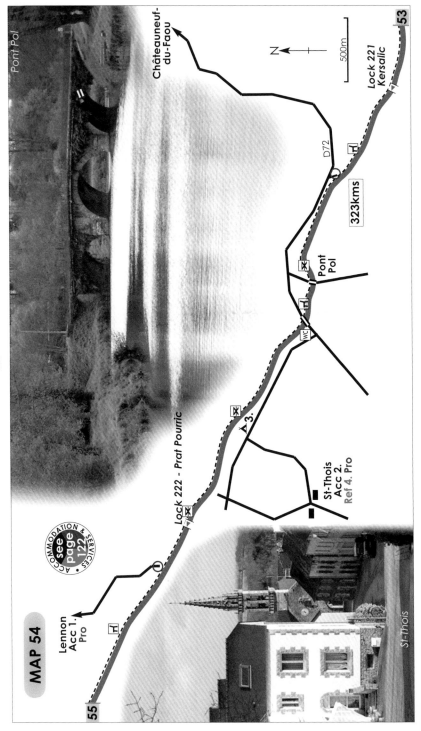

MAP 54

Pont Pol

Châteauneuf-
du-Faou

Lock 221
Kersalic

N

500m

D72

323kms

Pont
Pol

WC

Lock 222 - Prat Pourric

St-Thois
Acc 2.
Ref 4. Pro

A 3.

ACCOMMODATION & SERVICES
see page 122

Lennon
Acc 1.
Pro

St-Thois

55

53

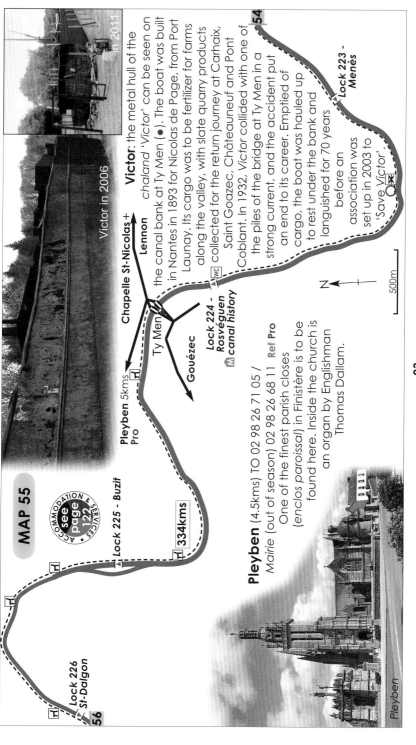

MAP 55

see page 122 — ACCOMMODATION & SERVICES

Lock 226 St-Dalgon

56

Lock 225 - Buzit

334kms

Lock 224 - Rosvéguen
🅼 canal history

Gouézec

Ty Men

Chapelle St-Nicolas+
Lennon

Pleyben 5kms
Pro

Victor in 2006

In 2011

Victor: the metal hull of the chaland 'Victor' can be seen on the canal bank at Ty Men (●). The boat was built in Nantes in 1893 for Nicolas de Page, from Port Launay. Its cargo was to be fertilizer for farms along the valley, with slate quarry products collected for the return journey at Carhaix, Saint Goazec, Châteauneuf and Pont Coblant. In 1932, Victor collided with one of the piles of the bridge at Ty Men in a strong current, and the accident put an end to its career. Emptied of cargo, the boat was hauled up to rest under the bank and languished for 70 years before an association was set up in 2003 to 'Save Victor'.

🅰 wc

Lock 223 - Menès

54

N

500m

Pleyben (4.5kms) TO 02 98 26 71 05 / *Mairie* (out of season) 02 98 26 68 11 **Ref Pro**
One of the finest parish closes (*enclos paroissal*) in Finistère is to be found here. Inside the church is an organ by Englishman Thomas Dallam.

Pleyben

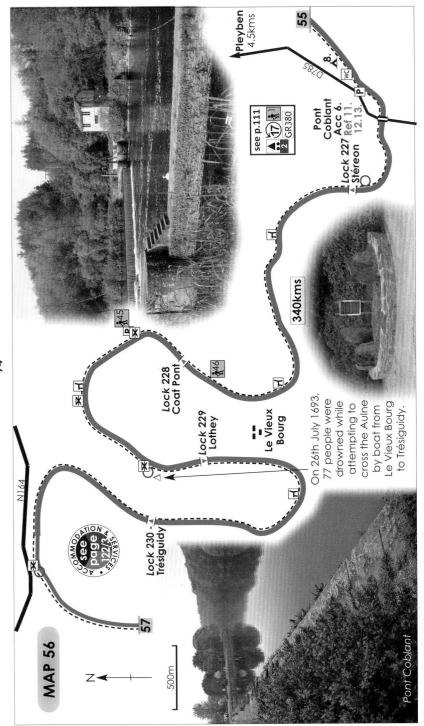

MAP 56

N

500m

N164

57

Lock 230 Trésiguidy

ACCOMMODATION & SERVICES · see page 122/3

On 26th July 1693, 77 people were drowned while attempting to cross the Aulne by boat from Le Vieux Bourg to Trésiguidy.

Le Vieux Bourg

Lock 229 Lothey

Lock 228 Coat Pont

D 45

46

340kms

see p.111
2 17
GR380

Lock 227 Stéreon

Pont Coblant Acc 6. Ref 11. 12.13.

Pleyben 4.5kms

D785

WC P

8.

55

Pont Coblant

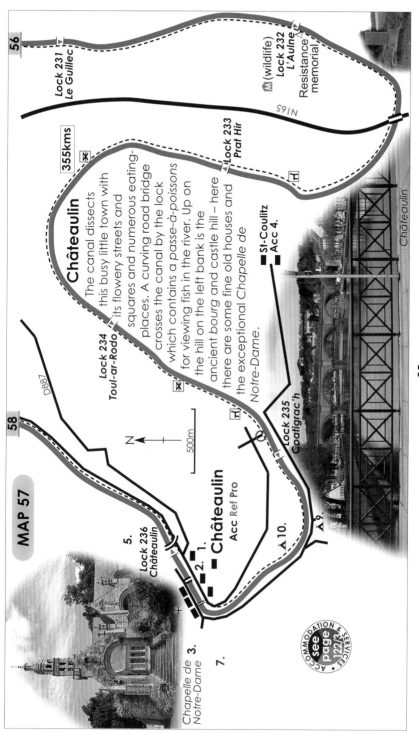

Lock 231
Le Guillec

M (wildlife)
Lock 232
L'Aulne
Resistance
memorial

N165

355kms

Châteaulin

The canal dissects
this busy little town with
its flowery streets and
squares and numerous eating-
places. A curving road bridge
crosses the canal by the lock
which contains a passe-à-poissons
for viewing fish in the river. Up on
the hill on the left bank is the
ancient bourg and castle hill – here
there are some fine old houses and
the exceptional Chapelle de
Notre-Dame.

Lock 234
Toul-ar-Rodo

Lock 233
Prat Hir

Lock 235
Coatigrac'h

St-Coulitz
Acc 4.

Châteaulin

D887

MAP 57

N

500m

5.

Lock 236
Châteaulin

2. 1.

Châteaulin
Acc Ref Pro

10.

9.

Chapelle de
Notre-Dame

3.

7.

ACCOMMODATION & SERVICES
see page 122/3.

95

MAP 58

St-Sébastien
chapel+

SEE
see
page
123
ACCOMMODATION & SERVICES

N165

N

500m

365kms

Lock 237
Guily Glas

barrage

Port Launay
Ref Pro

Acc 1.

57

The little bourg of **Port Launay** has an old-fashioned air in its graceful and serene setting on the canal before the last lock at Guily Glas.

GUILY GLAS

To avoid serious flooding such as that of 2000, when more than four hundred houses and businesses were inundated, a new barrage, unique in Europe, has been constructed at **Guily Glas** to regulate the flow of the Aulne by means of three horizontal valves controlled by sensors and hydraulic jacks.

The new barrage incorporates a *passe-à-poissons* composed of successive chambers equipped with valves to create the flow of water needed to attract the fish. A more direct route through the pass is provided for elvers.

The viaduct carries the railway, opened in December 1867, linking Quimper to Brest via Landerneau.

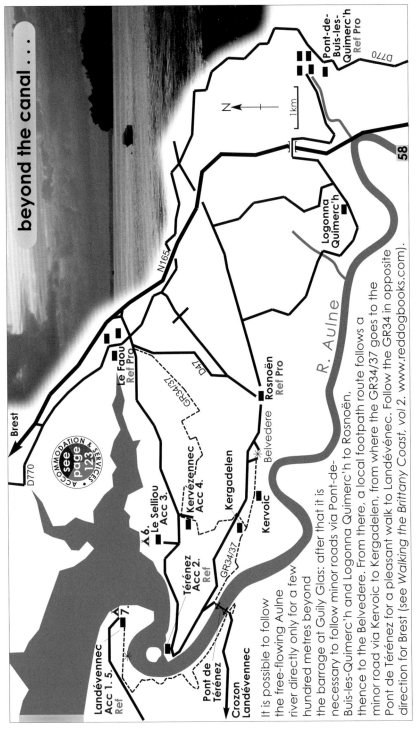

beyond the canal . . .

Pont-de-Buis-les-Quimerc'h *Ref Pro*

D770

1km

N

Logonna Quimerc'h

R. Aulne

58

Brest

D770

Le Faou *Ref Pro*

N165

D47

GR34/37

Rosnoën *Ref Pro*

Belvedere

Kervoic

Kergadelen

GR34/37

ACCOMMODATION & SERVICES · see page 123

Le Selliou Acc 3.

Å6.

Kervézennec Acc 4.

Térénez Acc 2. *Ref*

Landévennec Acc 1. 5. *Ref*

7.

Pont de Térénez

Crozon Landévennec

It is possible to follow the free-flowing Aulne river directly only for a few hundred metres beyond the barrage at Guily Glas: after that it is necessary to follow minor roads via Pont-de-Buis-les-Quimerc'h and Logonna Quimerc'h to Rosnoën, thence to the Belvedere. From there, a local footpath route follows a minor road via Kervoic to Kergadelen, from where the GR34/37 goes to the Pont de Térénez for a pleasant walk to Landévenec. Follow the GR34 in opposite direction for Brest (see *Walking the Brittany Coast, vol 2.* www.reddogbooks.com).

Landévennec

The ancient abbey of Landévennec, founded by Guénolé at the end of the 5th century, has an idyllic setting by the water, where the Aulne estuary pours out towards the Rade de Brest.

Forêt de Landévennec

From the bridge it is possible to walk all the way to Landévennec through the forests that belonged to the ancient abbey. The pretty *Chapelle du Folgoat* commemorates the legend of the simpleton whose only words 'Ave Maria' miraculously appeared on a lily growing from his grave.

Pont de Térénez

The Pont de Térénez was originally built in the 1920s, but the Germans blew it up to halt the Allied advance in 1944 and it did not reopen until 1952. This new, award-winning bridge has now replaced it.

... to Brest

For accommodation in Brest:
Tourist Office 02 98 44 24 96
www.brest-metropole-tourisme.fr

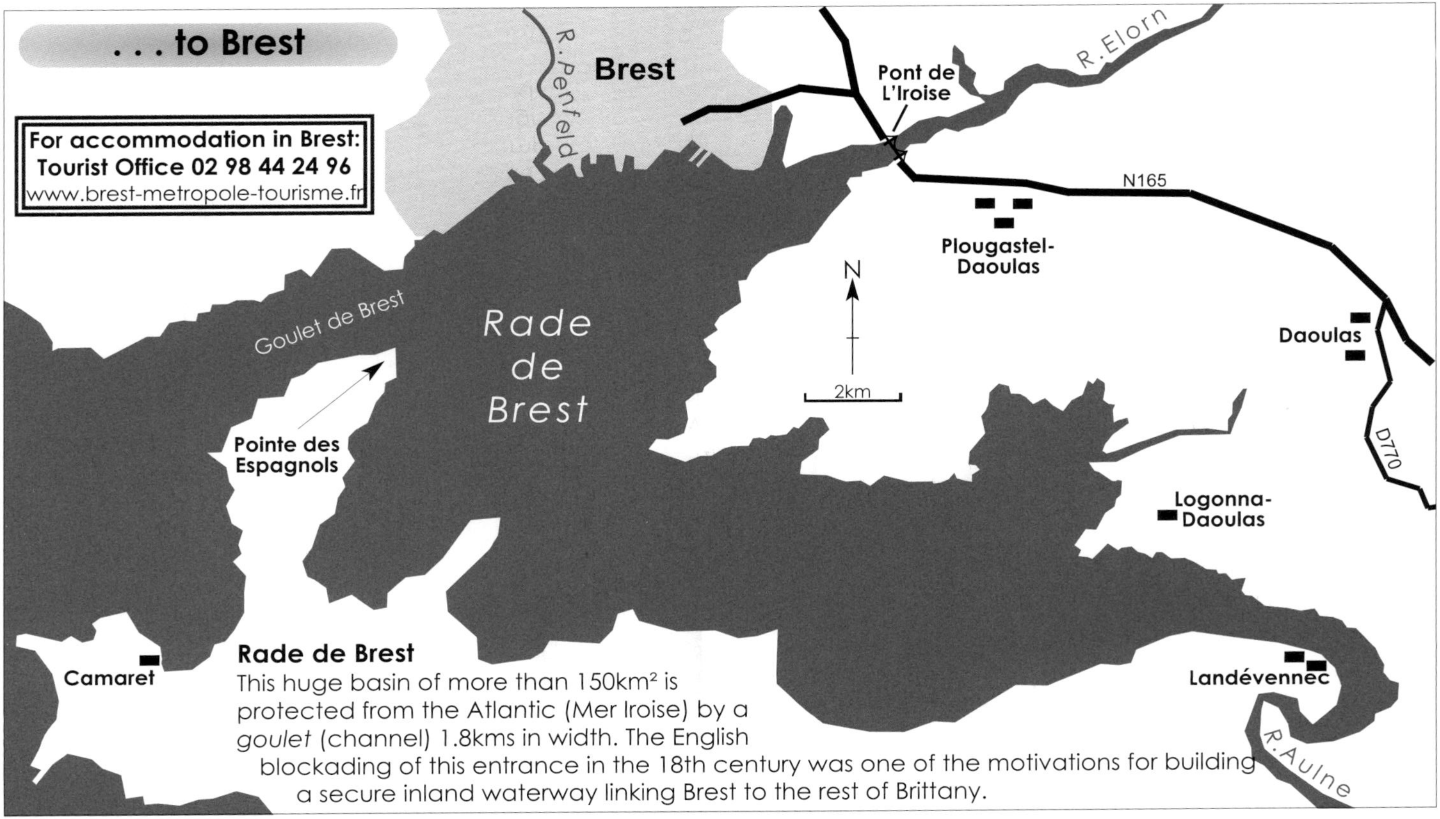

Brest

R.Penfeld

R.Elorn

Pont de
L'Iroise

N165

Plougastel-
Daoulas

Daoulas

D770

Logonna-
Daoulas

Landévennec

R.Aulne

N

2km

Rade
de
Brest

Goulet de Brest

Pointe des
Espagnols

Camaret

Rade de Brest

This huge basin of more than 150km² is
protected from the Atlantic (Mer Iroise) by a
goulet (channel) 1.8kms in width. The English
blockading of this entrance in the 18th century was one of the motivations for building
a secure inland waterway linking Brest to the rest of Brittany.

BREST

Brest was originally the site of a Roman *castellum*, but it was not earmarked as a significant settlement until the 13th century when it came into the possession of the Dukes of Brittany. In the wars of succession a hundred years later it was taken and held by the English until Richard II returned the town to Brittany in 1397.

Brest, from across the Rade

Cardinal Richlieu, governor of Brittany from 1626, was the first to develop the potential of the city as the main military port for the Atlantic seaboard, and in 1681 Brest replaced St-Renan as the regional capital.

Brest

The Tour Tanguy, a restored 14th century tower on the west bank of the Penfeld river now houses a museum of the history of Brest.

Louis XIV's chief engineer Vauban had a hand in organizing the city's defensive systems, but it was Choquet de Lindu who made the greatest mark here in the second half of the 18th century. He was responsible for developing the huge arsenal, on both banks of the Penfeld, for building and arming ships. Securing supplies for this establishment was one of the original purposes in the concept of the canal: at its height it employed up to 10,000 people. In 1750 the *bagne* (prison) was built and this later furnished the convicts who were sent to construct the Grande Tranchée of the Nantes-Brest canal at Glomel.

101

Walks and Cycle Rides

Many waymarked walks and cycle rides make use of the canal towpath to complete their circuit. The points at which they leave the towpath are marked on the canal maps with an appropriate symbol and a number for cross-referencing to this list. Please note that circuits and signage are liable to change.

A very brief outline of each circuit is given here, with an indication of where to find more complete directions and maps.

Note: other waymarks may exist that bear no relation to the walks and rides listed here. They are likely to be local circuits for which no published information is readily available, temporary waymarks for specific events, or obsolete.

MAP 1

Circuit des Marais de Blanche Noë 18km, clockwise (short-cut possible). Starts in Nort and joins the canal 800m from Lock 2 Quiheix. Crosses at the lock and returns on the *contre-halage* to cross over the first bridge and follow the towpath to a point 800m beyond Lock 3 La Tindière (MAP 2) before returning to Nort. More information: www.cceg.fr or TO Nort-sur-Erdre www.nort-sur-erdre.fr

Circuit de Vive Eve 5km, clockwise. Starts at the D26 bridge by the *contre-halage* northwards to cross at Lock 3 La Tindière (MAP 2) and continue on the towpath northwards for 800m. Here it turns off and briefly follows the same route as before returning to the canal, taking the towpath southwards to the starting point. More information: www.cceg.fr

MAP 2 Nort-sur-Erdre

Circuit des Marais de Blanche Noë
See under MAP 1

Circuit de Vive Eve
See under MAP 1

MAP 3

Circuit de l'Ecluse du Pas d'Heric, 8kms, signed both ways, so it leaves the canal either via the Rigole de Vioreau, west of Lock 7 - Pas d'Heric, or near the bridge over the canal to the east of Lock 7. Explores the Rigole and its hinterland. More information: www.cceg.fr

Circuit du Canal - Sentier de Bout de Bois 11km, easy, cyclable. Starts at the Plage de Bout de Bois (MAP 4). A circuit closely following the canal by the towpath and the *contre-halage* between Bout de Bois and the D39 crossing (MAP 3). More information: www.cceg.fr.

MAP 4 La Chevallerais

La Chevallerais - Circuit du Canal. 14km. Starts at church in La Chevallerais, joins canal west of Lock 8 La Remaudais and crosses at the lock. Re-crosses at the next bridge eastwards, loops around the north of La Chevallerais to rejoin the canal east of the *Halte Nautique* and return to the church. More information: TO Blain otsi.blain.free.fr

Circuit du Canal - Sentier de Bout de Bois
See under MAP 3

Héric - Circuit du Bourg au Canal 14km, cyclable. Starts in centre of Héric and makes for the canal just west of the N137 bridge. Follows towpath west and leaves southwards at the first bridge (where the towpath crosses) More information: www.cceg.fr or TO Nort-sur-Erdre www.nort-sur-erdre.fr.

MAP 5 Blain

Circuit du Perche 12km, anti-clockwise. Starts from the Port de Blain, following the towpath towards Nantes as far as Le Terrier, then north to La Mercerais and returning through Blain town centre. More information and map: TO Blain otsi.blain.free.fr

⚞8 Circuit des Sites 8km, clockwise. Starts from the Port de Blain, crossing the passerelle towards the château and continuing southwards, returning by a more westerly route to the canal at Lock 12 Paudais (MAP 6) and along the *contre-halage* to the start. More information and map: TO Blain otsi.blain.free.fr

⚞9 Circuit des Carrières 14km, clockwise. Starts from the Port de Blain, crossing the passerelle towards the château and taking the *contra-halage* westwards for about 4kms before turning south. Return to canal along former railway, then along the *contre-halage* to the start. More information and map: TO Blain 02 40 87 15 11 otsi.blain.free.fr

MAP 7

10 GRP (*Grandes Randonnées de Pays*)
Les Trois Rivières - circuit to the east of Redon, going from the Vilaine to the Don, the town of Guéméné-Penfao, then south through the Forêt du Gavre to Blain and returning by the canal. More information: TO Redon 02 99 71 06 04 www.tourisme-pays-redon.com

MAP 8

10 GRP (*Grandes Randonnées de Pays*)
Les Trois Rivières - see under MAP 7

MAP 9   Guenrouet

⑰ **Velo Promenade 17**, **Circuit de Plessé**, 24km, anti-clockwise, medium "blue". Starts at the Étang de Buhel near Plessé, joins the canal north of Guenrouet to follow the towpath towards Nantes for 5kms before returning towards Plessé. More information: TO Redon 02 99 71 06 04 www.tourisme-pays-redon.com

⚞1 Circuit de la Pierre Folle Menhir 10km, anticlockwise. Starts at the bridge to Guenrouet, following towpath eastwards for 1.5km. Leaves towpath towards village of Landron and rejoins canal west of Guenrouet at Port Tressé (MAP 10). More information: TO Redon 02 99 71 06 04 www.tourisme-pays-redon.com

MAP 10   Marais de Marongle

⚞2 Circuit de Coisnauté 11.5km, anticlockwise. Starts from near Coisnauté and immediately makes for the canal, and although this track is subject to flooding in winter, the circuit is practicable from the towpath further east (where marked on map) and from there loops round to the north of Coisnauté to rejoin the canal further west (MAP 11). More information: TO Redon 02 99 71 06 04 www.tourisme-pays-redon.com

MAP 11   Pont Miny

10 GRP (*Grandes Randonnées de Pays*)
Les Trois Rivières - see under MAP 7

MAP 12 & 13   Bellion

⑳ **Velo Promenade 20**, Circuit de Redon Sud, 29km, clockwise, medium "blue". Starts from Redon (TO) and follows the canal, initially on the *contre-halage,* east to Bellion, then south by minor roads to cross the Vilaine near Théhillac, returning to Redon up the right bank of the Vilaine. More information: TO Redon 02 99 71 06 04 www.tourisme-pays-redon.com

10 GRP (*Grandes Randonnées de Pays*)
Les Trois Rivières - see under MAP 7

MAP 14   Redon

⑳ **Velo Promenade 20**, see under MAP 12 & 13

MAP 15

Circuit De la Belle Anguille au Bois de Bahurel 15km, anti-clockwise. Starts from the carpark near the TO in Redon and along the towpath of the R.Vilaine before striking off westwards to join, briefly, the Nantes-Brest Canal. More information: TO Redon 02 91 71 06 04
www.tourisme-pays-redon.com

MAP 16   St-Vincent-sur-Oust

Circuit VTT Le Potinais 9km, "blue". Starts at the camping Bains-sur-Oust (MAP 17), soon climbing to a viewpoint over the Île aux Pies; then taking a roundabout route to the canal at La Potinais. More information: TO Redon 02 91 71 06 04
www.tourisme-pays-redon.com

Circuit de St-Vincent-sur-Oust 20km or 32km, medium. Starts in centre of St-Vincent-sur-Oust, joins canal at bridge to west of Lock 19 (MAP 17), leaves at La Potinais for a loop northwards, returning to La Potinais and following the *contre-halage* towards Redon before diverting to St-Perreux and back to St-Vincent. More information: TO Redon 02 91 71 06 04
www.tourisme-pays-redon.com

Circuit entre Marais et Chapelles 17km, clockwise. Starts at the camping Bains-sur-Oust (MAP 17) and explores the area betweem La Potinais and the Île-aux-Pies, yellow waymarks. More information: TO Redon 02 91 71 06 04
www.tourisme-pays-redon.com

GR347 Long distance hiking trail from Redon to Josselin, linking with GR38 from Redon and GR37 to Josselin.

MAP 17   Île aux Pies

Circuit de Peillac variants 16 - 32km, energetic. Starts in Peillac bourg, joins canal west of Pont d'Oust, follows towpath east to Lock 20 Limur. More information: TO Redon 02 91 71 06 04
www.tourisme-pays-redon.com

Circuit le Chemin du Ronde 8.5km. Starts from Peillac (bourg) and joins canal at the carpark near Pont d'Oust (MAP 18). Follows canal eastwards making a figure-of-8 between the carpark and Lock 20 Limur, blue waymarks.
More information: bretagne-rando.com
For a slightly shorter version see *Walks in Morbihan* walk 10.

GR38 Long distance hiking trail from Douarnenez (Finistère) to Redon. More information: http://www.gr-infos.com

GR347 Long distance hiking trail from Redon to Josselin, linking with GR38 from Redon and GR37 to Josselin.

MAP 18

Circuit le Chemin du Ronde see under MAP 17

MAP 21   Malestroit

Velo Promenade 16 La boucle canal sud - voie verte 12km, easy. Starts at Lock 25 Malestroit and follows the canal, initially on the *contre-halage,* to the Green Way bridge (Pont de la Bagotaie) then follows the Green Way south, up to Gare de Malestroit, then down to the town and canal. More information: TO Malestroit 02 97 75 45 35   tourisme.ccvol.com

MAP 22

Velo Promenade 16 La boucle canal - voie verte - see under MAP 21

Velo Promenade 18 Circuit de l'Oust et de Lanvaux 24km, medium. Starts at Lock 25 Malestroit on the towpath northwards, leaving the canal shortly to climb to the Green Way and follow it south for about 3kms before taking minor roads to reach the canal near St-Congard, then on the towpath back to Malestroit. More information: TO Malestroit 02 97 75 45 35
tourisme.ccvol.com

🚶16 Sentier de la rivière (No.29) 15km, clockwise, easy. Starts at Lock 25 Malestroit following towpath to Lock 27 Lanée 2, then joins the Green Way northwards across the canal and returns through the valley of the Oust to Malestroit (see *Walks in Morbihan*, walk 33). More information: TO Malestroit 02 97 75 45 35 tourisme.ccvol.com

V3 Former railway converted to Green Way (*voie verte*). More information: *Brittany's Green Ways*, Red Dog Books www.reddogbooks.com

MAP 23 Le Roc St-André

🔄15 Velo Promenade 15 La boucle canal nord - voie verte 19km, easy. Starts at Gare de la Chapelle Caro, follows the Green Way southwards to the canal, returning on the towpath to Le Roc St-André, continues on to Quily, rejoins the Green Way northwards to the canal and back to start via the towpath. More information: TO Malestroit 02 97 75 45 35 tourisme.ccvol.com

GR347 Long distance hiking trail from Redon to Josselin, linking with GR38 from Redon and GR37 to Josselin.

MAP 24 Montertelot

🔄3 Velo Promenade 3 Montertelot - Monterrein (Ploërmel) 28km, medium. Starts at Montertelot bourg, join it at the road 50m from canal. More information: bretagne-rando.com (listed under Ploërmel)

🚶17 Circut du canal aux rochers 8.4km. Montertelot to Rochers de St-Méen and Chapelle de St-Méen. Starts in car-park or nearby pike spawning pond. More information and map on information panel in car park.

MAP 25

🚶18 Circuit des Croix 13km, anti-clockwise; VTT possible. Starts from Lock 31 Guillac, initially on towpath eastwards, then loops round through Guillac and La Ville Meno and back to the start. More information: TO Josselin 02 97 22 36 43 www.josselin-communaute.fr

🚶19 Circuit de St-Gobrien 14km anti-clockwise, VTT possible. Starts from the bridge at St-Gobrien (MAP 26), then via St-Servant and on to cross the canal on road bridge south of Guillac, then back to St-Gobrien initially by the towpath but soon diverting onto the GR37. More information: TO Josselin 02 97 22 36 43 www.josselin-communaute.fr

MAP 26 Josselin

🔄10 Velo Promenade 10 La Vallée du Sedon 19km, energetic. Starts at Trégranteur, to Coët Bugat, Manoir de Mongrenier. Crosses canal at Josselin and turns east along towpath. More information: TO Josselin 02 97 22 36 43 www.josselin-communaute.fr

🔄12 Velo Promenade 12 La Vallée de l'Oust 22km, moderate. Starts by canal at St Gobrien, over the bridge to St-Servant, on to Quily and rejoining the canal via the Green Way (V3), then back to St Gobrien on the towpath. More information: TO Josselin 02 97 22 36 43 www.josselin-communaute.fr

🔄13 Velo Promenade 13 La Vallée de l'Oust 18km, easy. Starts from the quay (between the lock and the chateau) at Josselin, follows the former railway (now a minor road) to Guillac and returns via the towpath from Lock 31 Guillac. More information: TO Josselin 02 97 22 36 43 www.josselin-communaute.fr

🔄14 Velo Promenade 14 De l'Oust au Ninian 30km, energetic. Starts from the quay (between the lock and the chateau) at Josselin, follows towpath to Lock 34 St-Jouan, then tours around La Croix Hélléan, la Chapelle de St-Maudet, Hélléan and La Grée Saint-Laurent, then back to Josselin. More information: TO Josselin 02 97 22 36 43 www.josselin-communaute.fr

🚶19 Circuit de St-Gobrien see under MAP 25

MAP 27

(9) **Velo Promenade 9.** 21km, moderate. Starts at Chapelle de Pomeleuc and immediately joins the canal at Lock 41 La Tertraie 1 (MAP 28), follows towpath to Lock 38 Rouvray, then completes the circuit via Lantillac and Lock 42 La Tertraie 2. More information: TO Josselin 02 97 22 36 43 www.josselin-communaute.fr

🚶20 **Circuit de Pomeleuc** 14km, can be cycled. Starts from Lock 38 - Rouvray via the towpath to Bocneuf-la-Rivière then out-and-back to Pomeleuc via the towpath as far as Lock 41 - La Tertraie 1. Continuing from Bocneuf to Lantillac, it then returns to Rouvray along the south side of the canal. Yellow waymarks. More information: TO Josselin 02 97 22 36 43 www.josselin-communaute.fr

GR37 long distance hiking trail from Vitré (Ille-et-Vilaine) to Pentrez Plage (Finistère). More information: www.gr-infos.com

MAP 28

(8) **Velo Promenade 8 De la Forêt de Lanouée au Canal de Nantes à Brest** 15km, easy. Starts at Chapelle de Pomeleuc (northeast from Lock 41 La Tertraie 1) then by road to Les Forges, joining the canal at Lock 45 Griffet (MAP 29) and following it back to Pomeleuc. More information: TO Josselin 02 97 22 36 43 www.josselin-communaute.fr

(9) **Velo Promenade 9.** see under MAP 27

🚶20 **Circuit de Pomeleuc** see under MAP 27

GR37 long distance hiking trail from Vitré (Ille-et-Vilaine) to Pentrez Plage (Finistère). More information: www.gr-infos.com

MAP 30   Abbaye de Timadeuc

🚶21 **Circuit de l'Abbaye** 4.5km, clockwise. Join the circuit at the cross, 70m up the road from Lock 50 Timadeuc and continue up the road. Yellow waymarks. More information TO Pontivy tourisme-pontivycommunaute.com

GR37 long distance hiking trail from Vitré (Ille-et-Vilaine) to Pentrez Plage (Finistère). More information: www.gr-infos.com

MAP 31   Rohan

🚶22 **Short walk around the town**, including the covered market and parish church, returning to canal near the campsite. More information: www.rohan.fr/pdf/circuit_rando_rohan.pdf

GR37 long distance hiking trail from Vitré (Ille-et-Vilaine) to Pentrez Plage (Finistère). More information: www.gr-infos.com

MAP 32

GR37 long distance hiking trail from Vitré (Ille-et-Vilaine) to Pentrez Plage (Finistère). More information: www.gr-infos.com

MAP 33   Rigole d'Hilvern

🚶23 **Circuit du Canal et de la Rigole d'Hilvern** 13km. Starts from the lake near the church in St-Gonnery, crosses the Rigole d'Hivern and rejoins it later to follow it to the canal at Lock 78 Bel-Air. Crosses the canal at Lock 72 Pont and recrosses at Lock 59 Boju (MAP 32) to follow towpath back to Lock 67 La Forêt, from where it returns to St-Gonnery. More information: map only www.stgonnery.fr

Circuit des Écluses, 7km, easy, cyclable. Starts at Place de l'Église, Gueltas, making for the canal at Lock 59 Boju (MAP 32), following towpath westwards. There is a loop from Lock 67 La Forêt to the Rigole d'Hilvern, rejoining the canal at Lock 72 Pont, on towpath back to Lock 67 and either retrace route to start or cross canal and go through forest to the D125 back to Gueltas. More information: map only www.gueltas.fr (*carte du randonneur*)

GR37 long distance hiking trail from Vitré (Ille-et-Vilaine) to Pentrez Plage (Finistère). More information: www.gr-infos.com

MAP 34

GR37 long distance hiking trail from Vitré (Ille-et-Vilaine) to Pentrez Plage (Finistère). More information: www.gr-infos.com

MAP 36

Pontivy community of communes does offer a selection of walking circuits, some of which are based on the canal, but information has not been available on-line until recently (walk cards have been uploaded to Flikr). A pack of walks or individual walk cards can be purchased from the Tourist Office in Pontivy, which can be found in the *péniche Duchesse Anne* moored on the Blavet, 2 quai Niémen, Pontivy. tourisme-pontivycommunaute.com

MAP 38

VD2 **Velo-route départementale 2**, Pontivy to Guémené-sur-Scorff.

MAP 39

Circuit du Blavet (The Blavet Trail) 12.7km, easy. Starts from le Corboulo, direction Botcol but soon diverting to St Aignan village (MAP 40). Crosses the footbridge to Lock 119 Guerlédan, then follows the towpath south as far as Boloré, returning via le Cloître and Trémer. Blue waymarks. This circuit links with two others to the west. More information: mairie, St-Aignan www.saint-aignan56.fr

MAP 40 St-Aignan

Circuit VTT de Malvran 29km anti-clockwise, "black". Starts at *Station VTT* at *Base Départementale de Plein Air de Guerlédan*. Route in the Forêt de Quénécan, south of Lac Guerlédan. More information: TO Mur-de-Bretagne 02 96 28 51 41 www.guerledan.fr or Base Plein Air de Guerlédan www.base-plein-air-guerledan.com

Circuit VTT Saint-Aignan - 28km anti-clockwise "blue". Starts at *Station VTT* at *Base Départementale de Plein Air de Guerlédan*. Explores the countryside surrounding St-Aignan, including a stretch of the canal. More information: TO Mur-de-Bretagne 02 96 28 51 41 www.guerledan.fr or Base Plein Air de Guerlédan www.base-plein-air-guerledan.com

GR341 long distance hiking trail from Bréhec (Côtes d'Armor) to Riantec (Morbihan). GR341S skirts the southern (Morbihan) side of Lac Guerlédan.

MAP 41 Lac Guerlédan

Circuit VTT de Bon Repos 36km anti-clockwise, "red". Starts at *Station VTT* at *Base Départementale de Plein Air de Guerlédan*. More information: TO Mur-de-Bretagne 02 96 28 51 41
www.guerledan.fr
or Base Plein Air de Guerlédan
/www.base-plein-air-guerledan.com

Circuit VTT de Caurel - 20km anti-clockwise, "green". Starts at *Station VTT* at *Base Départementale de Plein Air de Guerlédan*. More information: TO Mur-de-Bretagne 02 96 28 51 41
www.guerledan.fr or Base Plein Air de Guerlédan
www.base-plein-air-guerledan.com

Circuit de Lorette 35km anti-clockwise - VTT black. Starts at *Station VTT* at *Base Départementale de Plein Air de Guerlédan*. More information: TO Mur-de-Bretagne 02 96 28 51 41 www.guerledan.fr or Base Plein Air de Guerlédan
www.base-plein-air-guerledan.com

(6a) Balade de Caurel 7.5km Not so much a circuit, more a series of diversions from the Green Way towards the lake and into the village of Caurel. Waymarked (temporarily) thin white arrow on dk.green rectangle. *Fiche 6* of *'Balades à vélo autour de la voie verte du petit train'* from TOs in Côtes d'Armor. Map displayed at Gare de St-Gelven, and at Caurel. TO Mur-de-Bretagne 02 96 28 51 41

V6 Former railway converted to Green Way (*voie verte*). More information: *Brittany's Green Ways*, Red Dog Books www.reddogbooks.com

Bois de Caurel 8km. Starts from sports field in Caurel, clockwise. No.2 in *"Balades en Pays de Guerlédan-Argoat"* from TOs in Côtes d'Armor. TO Mur-de-Bretagne 02 96 28 51 41

Landes de Caurel 16km. Starts from Caurel church, finishes on same route as g. but in opposite direction. No.25 in *'Les Côtes d'Armor à pied'* (FFRP).

GR341 long distance hiking trail from Bréhec (Côtes d'Armor) to Riantec (Morbihan).

MAP 42 Bon Repos

Circuit VTT de Bon Repos
see under MAP 41

(6a) Balade de Caurel
see under MAP 41

(6b) **Balade de St-Gelven** 9.4km, easy but with some climbs. Starts at the church in St-Gelven but alternatively from Bon Repos. *Fiche 6* of *'Balades à vélo autour de la voie verte du petit train'* from TOs in Côtes d'Armor. TO Mur-de-Bretagne 02 96 28 51 41

(6c) Balade de St-Gelven/Perret 8km, easy. Starts at Bon Repos and visits Les Forges des Salles (recommended) and the Bois de Fao. *Fiche 6* of *'Balades à vélo autour de la voie verte du petit train'* from TOs in Côtes d'Armor. TO Mur-de-Bretagne 02 96 28 51 41

Landes de Liscuis 11km. Starts at Rosquelfen (nr. Gouarec) takes a clockwise route to the Gorges du Daoulas and returns via the Landes de Liscuis. No.3 in *"Balades en Pays de Guerlédan-Argoat"* from TOs in Côtes d'Armor. TO Mur-de-Bretagne 02 96 28 51 41

Bois de l'Abbaye 6.5km. Starts at Bon Repos, on path between the canal and the café de l'Abbaye. Yellow waymarks, Open 1st March to 30th September, map displayed near start.

Bois du Fao 4.2km. Starts at Bon Repos, on path from road on south side of canal. Yellow waymarks. Open 1st March to 30th September, map displayed near start.

GR341 long distance hiking trail from Bréhec (Côtes d'Armor) to Riantec (Morbihan).

GR37 long distance hiking trail, Vitré - Rohan - Pentrez Plage.

V6 Former railway converted to Green Way (*voie verte*). More information: *Brittany's Green Ways*, Red Dog Books www.reddogbooks.com

MAP 43 Gouarec

⚐31 Landes de Liscuis 12.5km. Starts from Gouarec TO (former station), clockwise, climbs to the Landes de Liscuis and its three Neolithic alley graves, descends to Bon Repos and returns through woods and along the canal. No.28 in *Walks in Côtes d'Armor* Red Dog Books www.reddogbooks.com

⚐32 Bois de Gouarec 14km. Starts at the Gare de Gouarec (TO, map of route displayed nearby). Anticlockwise circuit from, and back to this point on the canal. More information TO Gouarec or AIKB Gouarec www.aikb.fr

V6 Former railway converted to Green Way (*voie verte*). More information: *Brittany's Green Ways*, Red Dog Books www.reddogbooks.com
(Here the Green Way follows the canal as the line of the railway has been erased by the road, the former N164)

MAP 44 Coatnatous

ⓐ Plélauff to Lock 147 Restouel on the towpath, returning to Plélauff by the D76 (approx 12km). Waymarked anti-clockwise 🔳. Links with other longer circuits to give an extended tour of the area. General information: TO Rostrenen 02 96 29 02 72 tourismekreizbreizh.com.

⑦ Balade de Gouarec/Plélauff 8km, easy to medium. Waymarked 🔳. Starts at Lock 140 Gouarec, anti-clockwise, westwards along towpath to Plélauff bourg, returning across country by minor roads to the bridge at Gouarec. *Fiche 7* of *'Balades à vélo autour de la voie verte du petit train'* from TOs in Côtes d'Armor.

MAP 45 Pont Auffret

⑧ Balade de Rostrenen/Glomel 14km, energetic. Starts at the old station in Rostrenen (Green Way V6) joins canal (Map 46) between Locks 155 and 156, leaves across Lock 159 Quistinic, re-crosses canal at Lock 153 Kerriou to return to Rostrenen. Waymarks, thin white arrow on dk. green rectangle (or replaced by 🔳). *Fiche 8* of *'Balades à vélo autour de la voie verte du petit train'* from TOs in Côtes d'Armor.

⚐33 Moulin de Kerbescont 11km. Starts from Rostrenen. No.26 in *'Les Côtes d'Armor à pied'* (FFRP), or for a variant (10km) see *'Central Brittany, Coast to Coast'* (Red Dog Books) walk No.6. Yellow waymarks, or white & red on the GR.

GR37 long distance hiking trail, Vitré - Rohan - Pentrez Plage.

MAP 46 La Grande Tranchée

⑧ Balade de Rostrenen/Glomel see under MAP 45

⚐34 La Grande Tranchée 10km. Starts from the church in Glomel in the direction of the mairie. Take 1st left and follow red/white waymarks to canal, then blue. More information: No.8 in *"Balades en Pays de Guerlédan-Argoat"* from TOs in Côtes d'Armor or No.14 in *Walks in Côtes d'Armor* Red Dog Books www.reddogbooks.com

GR37 long distance hiking trail, Vitré - Rohan - Pentrez Plage.

GR38 Long distance hiking trail from Douarnenez (Finistère) to Redon. More information: http://www.gr-infos.com

MAP 48 Pont de Goariva

♦35 Le canal de Nantes à Brest
12.4 km, anti-clockwise. Starts at the church of St-Trémeur, Carhaix, anti-clockwise. Joins canal towpath via the Green Way V7 (MAP 49) and returns to Carhaix from Lock 196 Kergoutois. Blue waymarks. More information: TO Carhaix
www.huelgoat-carhaix-tourisme.com

♦36 Le Moustoir, "Loch Coucou" 6km, clockwise. Starts from the carpark opposite the church in Le Moustoir (east of Carhaix on old N164), joins canal near Lock 190 Moustoir and leaves it at Pont Goariva. Yellow waymarks. More information: TO Carhaix
www.huelgoat-carhaix-tourisme.com

GR37 long distance hiking trail, Vitré - Rohan - Pentrez Plage.

MAP 49 Port de Carhaix

♦37 Les ardoisières 16km anti-clockwise. Starts at Butte de la Cheval. Joins canal towpath from the south between Locks 199 and 200 and leaves it at Port de Carhaix. Yellow waymarks. More information: TO Carhaix
www.huelgoat-carhaix-tourisme.com

♦38 St-Hernin, L'Argoat 17km anti-clockwise. Starts by the mairie in St-Hernin, joins canal towpath at Port de Carhaix and follows it westwards to Lock 204 Coz Castel to continue westwards on the Green Way V6. Yellow waymarks. More info:TO Carhaix
www.huelgoat-carhaix-tourisme.com

V6 and V7 Former railways converted to Green Way (voie verte). More information: Brittany's Green Ways, Red Dog Books www.reddogbooks.com

MAP 50

♦39 Cleden-Poher, Circuit des fontaines 13kms Starts by the mairie, anti-clockwise to join the canal towpath between Locks 208 Lesnevès and 207 Le Ster. Follows towpath eastwards, passing Lock 206 then returning to Cleden-Poher bourg. Yellow waymarks. More information: TO Carhaix
www.huelgoat-carhaix-tourisme.com

V6 Former railway converted to Green Way (voie verte). More information: Brittany's Green Ways, Red Dog Books
www.reddogbooks.com

MAP 51 Pont Triffin

♦40 Cleden-Poher, Circuit de l'Aulne 20kms Starts from Place des Anciens Combattants, near the mairie, clockwise to join the canal towpath 2.5kms east of Pont Triffen. Follows towpath westwards, leaves at Pont Triffen to explore the river Aulne upstream before returning to Cleden-Poher bourg. Blue waymarks. More information: TO Carhaix
www.huelgoat-carhaix-tourisme.com

36 Tro Bro Landelo 24kms, VTT blue (easy). Starts in Landelau, joining canal at Pont Triffen. Re-crossing the N164 it traces the former railway for a few kilometres (including some Green Way) before leaving northwards to complete its circuit. More information: www.bases-vtt-29.fr
(Note: if travelling westwards, following this route initially but continuing on the railway line to the D236, then following that into Chateauneuf-du-Faou to rejoin the canal, is a shorter route than by the canal.)

V6 Former railway converted to Green Way (*voie verte*). More information: *Brittany's Green Ways*, Red Dog Books www.reddogbooks.com

MAP 53   Châteauneuf-du-Faou

🚶41 **Circuit PR No.1** 5km, clockwise. Starts from the *Centre des Vacances* on the south side of the canal at Châteanueuf, crosses by the old bridge and takes the towpath westwards (downstream) for 200m, then climbs the hillside to the town. More information: TO Châteauneuf-du-Faou www.chateauneuf-du-faou.com

🚶42 **Circuit PR No.2** 12km Starts from the Centre des Vacances on the south side of the canal at Châteanueuf, crosses by the old bridge and takes the towpath westwards (downstream) and leaves it by the next road off after Lock 220 Kerbaoret. More information: TO Châteauneuf-du-Faou 02 98 81 83 90 www.chateauneuf-du-faou.com

🚶43 **Circuit PR No.3** 8.5km Starts from the Centre des Vacances on the south side of the canal at Châteanueuf, crosses by the old bridge and bears right to follow minor roads and tracks over the hill to the canal further east, returning along the towpath to cross the canal at Lock 217 Boudrac'h, then reaching the canal west of Chateauneuf and following it back to Châteauneuf. More information: TO Châteauneuf-du-Faou www.chateauneuf-du-faou.com

🚶44 **Circuit PR No.4** 9.5km (*Circuit de la Chapelle du Moustoir*). Starts from the Centre des Vacances on the south side of the canal at Châteanueuf, crosses by the old bridge and bears right to follow minor roads and tracks over the hill to le Moustoir, returning along the towpath to the first road on the right, then across country to Châteanueuf. Green waymarks. more information: TO Châteauneuf-du-Faou www.chateauneuf-du-faou.com

MAP 56   Pont Coblant

🚶45 **Circuit de Maner Coz** 13km anti-clockwise. Starts from the church in Pleyben, direction St-Ségal, passing Chapelle St-Laurent and Maner Coz (the old manor of Tresiguidy) before descending to the canal. Yellow waymarks. More information: TO Pleyben 02 98 26 71 05 www.mairiepleyben.fr/~tourisme

🚶46 **Circuit de Pont Coblant** 8km, clockwise. Starts from Pont Coblant following towpath westwards. Yellow waymarks. More information: TO Pleyben 02 98 26 71 05 www.mairiepleyben.fr/~tourisme See *Walks in Finistere*, Red Dog Books www.reddogbooks.com

Accommodation - Refreshments - Provisions

(all distances are from the canal)

MAPS 1 & 2

ACCOMMODATION

Hotels

1. Hôtel Relais de la Grange (5kms)
Nort-sur-Erdre 02 12 60 57
www.relaislagrange.com

2. Hôtel du Commerce (3kms)
Nort-sur-Erdre 02 40 72 20 53

Chambres d'hôte

3. M.Bernard Fourage (3kms) 1 route
d'Issé, Nort-sur-Erdre 02 40 72 21 03
lemarais44@yahoo.fr
2 rooms Open all year

4. Marie-Claude Courant (3kms)
Sucé-sur-Erdre 02 40 77 99 61
www.lagamotrie.com 3 rooms
Swimming pool Open all year

Gîte d'Etape

5. Gîte d'Etape de Vault (8kms)
02 40 72 10 49   18 places Open all
year gite.nort-sur-erdre@orange.fr

Camping

6. Camping du Port Mulon (municipal
site), Rue des Mares Noires, Nort-sur-
Erdre 70 places Mar to Oct
02 40 72 23 57
Camping.nort-sur-erdre@orange.fr

REFRESHMENTS

Nort-sur-Erdre – restaurants, cafés,
bars

Sucé-sur-Erdre – restaurants, cafés,
bars

PROVISIONS

Nort-sur-Erdre – all shops and
services

Sucé-sur-Erdre – all shops and
services

MAPS 3 & 4

ACCOMMODATION

Hotels

1. Hotel Restaurant l'Abreuvoir (3kms)
La Croix Blanche, Héric
02 40 57 63 81
www.restaurant-abreuvoir.com

Gîte d'Etape

2 Les Hirondelles (2kms)
La Heurtaudais, Héric 02 40 57 67 06
bsmlpinel@wanadoo.fr
http://gite-des-
hirondelles.pagesperso-orange.fr

Camping

3. M.& Mme Robert (3kms) La Foué,
44130 Blain 02 40 79 19 91
April – Nov Place in caravan per
night possible

REFRESHMENTS

3. La Chevallerais - Café du Stade

4. Bout-de-Bois - Restaurant Le
Baloutyn 02 40 57 62 52

5. Café-Restaurant Le Canal
02 40 57 60 54 Open for lunch

PROVISIONS

La Chevallerais – grocery, bakery,
bank/cash point

MAPS 5 & 6

ACCOMMODATION

Hotels

1. Hotel-Brasserie Le Grand Cerf
(800m) Blain 02 40 79 00 47
12 rooms

2. Hotel La Gerbe de Blé (500m)
4, place Jean Guihard, Blain
09 83 80 83 94 gerbdeble.fr

Chambres d'hôte

3. Mme Hecaud (300m) Le Gravier
02 40 79 10 25 3 rooms

4. M&Mme Pineau (3kms)
La Mercerais, Blain 02 40 79 04 30   2
rooms

Gîte d'Etape

5. La Groulais (near canal) TO Blain
02 40 87 15 11 or 06 88 34 72 38

Camping

6. Camping du Château (by canal)
Blain 02 40 79 11 00 May – end Sept

REFRESHMENTS

A wide choice of restaurants,
crêperies and cafés in Blain.

PROVISIONS

All shops and services in Blain.

MAPS 7 & 8

ACCOMMODATION

Chambres d'hôte

1. Le Nid d'Omer (150m) Dominique et Eric OYER, La Rouaudais, 44130 St-Omer-de-Blain 02 40 51 35 38 or 06 66 79 00 89 www.lenidomer.fr

REFRESHMENTS

2. Bougard Crêperie aux berges de Bougard (by canal) 02 40 79 07 05 (closed Mon/Tues)

Saint-Omer de Blain (1km north of the canal) Restaurant, café,

Notre-Dame de Grâce (1km south of the canal) Café

PROVISIONS

Saint-Omer de Blain - grocery and *dépôt pain*, bank/cash point

Notre-Dame de Grâce (1km south of the canal) Bakery and *dépôt pain*

MAPS 9 & 10

ACCOMMODATION

Chambres d'hôte

1. Mme Biard (5kms) Le Cougou, Guenrouet 02 40 79 49 30 www.lecougou.com Open all year

2. Mme Lasausse (5kms) Le Cougou, Guenrouet 02 40 87 79 09 Open all year http://excareve.free.fr

Gîte d'Etape

3. Halte Nautique (by canal) Guenrouet mairie 02 40 87 64 18 May – Sept 6 places

4. La Rivière Blanche (2.5kms) La Touche-Robin, Guenrouet 02 40 87 64 94 http://rb44.free.fr Open all year (14 places)

Camping

5. Camping Saint-Clair (by canal) Guenrouet 02 40 87 61 52 mid Apr – end Sept Place in caravan per night possible chabliny@wanadoo.fr

REFRESHMENTS

Guenrouet – restaurant, café, bar

6. Crêperie du Port PK 73 (by canal) Guenrouet June-Sept 02 40 87 69 00

PROVISIONS

Guenrouet – grocery, bakery, delicatessen, bank/cash point

MAPS 11, 12 & 13

ACCOMMODATION

Chambres d'hôte

1. Au Petit Nid Douillet (4km from Pont Miny) 35 Rétaud, Guenrouet 02 44 04 08 80 or 06 22 20 37 31 Open all year www.aupetitniddouillet.fr

Gîte d'Etape

2. Maison du Canal (by canal) Pont Miny 02 40 91 24 96 or 06 85 57 51 97 (mairie) 10 places, kitchen facilities. Open all year

Camping

3. Camping du Bellion (by canal) 02 40 91 20 21 (mairie) May - end Sept

REFRESHMENTS

4. Fégréac Le Bistrot Gourmand 02 40 91 27 34 Lunch time

Also a bar and café in Fégréac.

PROVISIONS

Fégréac – food store, bakery, butcher, bank/cash point.

MAPS 14 & 15

ACCOMMODATION

Hotels

1. Bel Hotel (200m) St-Nicolas-de-Redon 33 rooms 02 99 71 10 10 bel-hotel.com

2. Hotel Le France (by canal) 30 rue DuGuesclin, Redon 02 99 71 06 11 www.hotellefrance.com

3. Asther Hotel (near canal) 14 rue des Douves 02 99 71 10 91 www.asther-hotel.com

4. Hotel Chandouineau (400m) 1 rue Thiers 02 99 71 02 04
www.hotel-restaurant-chandouineau.com

5. Ibis Budget Hotel (2kms) 7 rue Louis Guillou 08 92 70 12 59
www.accorhotels.com

Chambres d'hôte

6. La Maison Jaune (500m) M&Mme Hulbert 31 Rue de Vannes, Redon
3 rooms Open all year
02 99 72 16 59 or 06 85 84 51 75
http://redon-maisonjaune.blogspot.fr

7 Mme Houel (3.5kms) 58 rue de La Riaudais, 35600 Redon 02 99 72 35 70
lariaudaie.com

Camping

8. M. Mme. Guerin (1.5km) La Morinais, 35600 Bains-sur-Oust
02 99 72 12 17 Open Mar - Nov
www.fermelamorinais.com

REFRESHMENTS

A range of options in St-Nicolas and Redon, many near the canal.

PROVISIONS

A full range of shops and services in St-Nicolas and Redon, including Super-U and Leclerc supermarkets in close proximity to the canal.

MAPS 16 & 17

ACCOMMODATION

1. Ferme équestre/Rando-Gîte (1.7kms) Ménéhy 02 99 91 35 15
Camping/rooms (24 places)
Open all year Horses
gitedumenehy.wordpress.com

Chambres d'hôte

2. Château de Sourdeac (4kms - possibility of pick up from canal and back again next morning)
56200 Glénac 02 99 08 13 64
www.sourdeac.fr 2 rooms
Open Easter to end Oct.

Camping

3. Camping Municipal (by Oust) L'Ile aux Pies 02 99 91 71 41 Mid June-mid-Sept 60 places bainssuroust.net

4. Camping Le Painfaut (500m) St-Vincent-sur-Oust 06 88 64 69 87
www.camping-lepainfaut.fr
30-places Open all year

REFRESHMENTS

5. St-Vincent-sur-Oust Restaurant Au Fil de l'Oust (Route de l'Ile aux Pies, by canal) 02 99 91 37 21 May-Sept.

Saint-Vincent-sur-Oust - café, bar and crêperie

PROVISIONS

Saint-Vincent-sur-Oust – grocery and bakery

MAPS 18 & 19

ACCOMMODATION

Hotels

1. Hotel-Restaurant Chez Antoine (1.5kms) Peillac 02 99 91 24 43
8 rooms
hotel-chez-antoine.pagesperso-orange.fr

2. Hotel-Restaurant Le Rivage (1.5kms) Peillac 02 99 91 33 78 Meals midday 5 rooms

3. Hotel-Restaurant du Guélin (by canal) St-Martin-sur-Oust
02 99 91 55 90 12 rooms

Chambres d'hôte

4. Château de Castellan (2.5kms) M. et Mme Cossé St-Martin-sur-Oust
02 99 91 51 69
http://auberge.perso.sfr.fr

5. La Grange aux Moines (by canal) 02 97 43 54 71 Reservations out of season possible 7 rooms Swimming pool Horses

Camping

8. Camping Municipal (by canal) Le Pont d'Oust, 56220 Peillac
02 99 91 26 76 (mairie)
mairie@peillac.fr May to Sept

9. Camping Municipal La Digue (by canal) St-Martin-sur-Oust
02 99 91 55 76 78 places May - Sept

REFRESHMENTS

10. Pont d'Oust Bar/restaurant La Ciboulette (near canal)
02 99 71 45 71

11. Peillac Crêperie La Breizhoise (1.5kms) Place de l'Eglise 02 99 91 26 50 Closed Mondays

12. Le Guelin Crêperie Chez Bernard (near canal) 02 99 91 53 84 Midday only out of season

PROVISIONS

Peillac (1.2kms) Supermarket, grocery, bakery, bars, PO, bank/cash point

St-Martin-sur-Oust (400m) Cafe, grocery, bakery, bank/cash point

MAPS 20 & 21

ACCOMMODATION
Hotels

1. Hotel Cap-Horn (300m) Malestroit 02 97 75 13 01 7 rooms www.hotel-malestroit.com

Chambres d'hôte

2. M&Mme Gru (1.5kms) La Brière St-Laurent-sur-Oust 02 97 75 02 62 3 rooms Use of kitchen Open all year

Gîte d'étape - Rando Plume

3. Les Laurentides (300m from new *passerelle*)Jean-Claude Nizan, St-Laurent-sur-Oust 02 97 73 78 36 Use of kitchen Horses Open all year www.les-laurentides.fr

4. Gîte d'étape Ecluse (by canal) Malestroit 02 97 75 11 75 (mairie) 24 places Open April to Oct

Camping

5. Camping Municipal de la Daufresne (by canal) Malestroit 06 83 69 88 17 75 places Open May to September

6. Camping du Halage (by canal) Saint-Congard 35 places 02 97 43 50 13 June to Sept

REFRESHMENTS

7. Saint-Congard Bar Le Canal Open in season

8. Saint-Laurent-sur-Oust Restaurant Le Tono du Village 02 97 75 17 05

Malestroit has a good selection of restaurants, pizzerias, crêperies, cafés and bars.

PROVISIONS

Saint-Congard (by canal) Bakery, grocery

Saint-Laurent-sur-Oust (400m) Bakery, grocery, bars

Malestroit (by canal) - all shops and services

MAPS 22 & 23

ACCOMMODATION
Hotels

1. Hotel-Restaurant Le Petit Kériquel (1.5kms) La Chapelle-Caro 02 97 74 82 44 lepetitkeriquel@orange.fr 5 rooms www.keriquel.com

Camping

2. Camping Le Domaine du Roc (by canal) Le Roc-Saint-André 02 97 74 91 07 April to Sept 50 places Tree-top cabins/ chalets also available www.domaine-du-roc.com

REFRESHMENTS

3. Relais des Routiers, La Gare (300m) Bar-restaurant / Buffet 02 97 74 93 47

4. Le Roc-Saint-André La Chaumière (100m) Bar-crêperie-grill 02 97 74 94 09

PROVISIONS

La Chapelle-Caro – bakery, grocery, bar

Le Roc-Saint-André - bakery, grocery, bars, bank/cash point

MAPS 24 & 25

ACCOMMODATION
Chambres d'hôte

1. M&Mme Adelys (5kms) Le Temple, 56120 Saint-Servant 02 97 22 34 33 1 room Open all year

2. Brigitte Min Kim (300m) An Ti Coz, Caruhel, 56800 Guillac 09 67 10 18 51 or 06 83 04 17 81 anticoz.fr

3 Les Ecuries du Crévy (150m) 56460 La Chapelle-Caro gîtes & chambres d'hôte lecrevy.com

REFRESHMENTS

4. Montertelot Bar-Grill de l'Ecluse
02 97 74 85 91

5. L'Escale snack bar, Montertelot
02 97 74 91 31

6. La Ville Nayl Crêperie La Gavotte
02 97 74 81 19 Easter to September

7. Quily Bar-restaurant Le Liqui-Liqui
02 97 74 98 66 (also grocery, *dépôt pain*)

8. Saint-Servant Restaurant-Bar
L'Excalibur 02 97 75 63 65 Midday meals

Guillac bar, café

PROVISIONS

Montertelot Bar, *dépôt pain*

Quily – see 7. above

Guillac – bakery, grocery, bar, café

Saint-Servant – bakery

MAPS 26 & 27

ACCOMMODATION

Hotels

1. Hotel-restaurant du Château (by canal) Josselin 36 rooms
02 97 22 20 11
www.hotel-chateau.com

2. Hotel-restaurant Rive Gauche
(100m) 87 rue Glatinier. Josselin (rear access to towpath) 7 rooms
02 97 75 63 36

3. Hotel-restaurant Le Relais de l'Oust
(by canal) 25 rooms 02 97 75 63 06
Open all year
www.aurelaisdeloust.com

Chambres d'hôte

4. M&Mme Le Goff (400m) 14 rue
St-Michel, Josselin 5 rooms
02 97 22 24 24 / 06 89 37 26 07
contact@le14stmichel.com
www.le14stmichel.com

5. Jean & Marie Guyot (500m)
Chemin de la Butte St-Laurent,
Josselin 4 rooms Use of kitchen April
to Sept 02 97 22 22 09
chez.guyot@chambres-bretagne.com
www.chambres-bretagne.com

6. Mme Ann Bird (400m) 6 rue de
Caradec, 56120 Josselin
02 97 73 98 07 / 06 27 52 85 28
bbird64@gmail.com

7. Les Hortensias (3kms) M&Mme
Nicolas La Ville Robert, La Croix
Hélléan 02 97 75 64 37 3 rooms
leshortensias.net

Gîte d'étape

8. Maison Eclusière Josselin
02 97 22 24 17 (mairie)
mairie@josselin.com May to end of
Sept 14 places Use of kitchen

Camping

9. Camping des Cerisiers (800m)
M&Mme Turac Brancillet
02 97 75 61 24 Room in caravan
possible Horses Open all year
contact@josselincamping.com

10. Le Domaine de Kerelly (500m)
Guegon 02 97 22 22 20 55 places
Rooms in caravan April to end of
October camping-josselin.com

REFRESHMENTS

Josselin has a good selection of
restaurants and crêperies, in addition
to hotel facilities.

**11. Hotel-restaurant Le Relais de
l'Oust** by Ecluse 38 Rouvray (see Acc
above)

12. Bar Brasserie Le Bocneuf (near
canal) 02 97 75 35 86

PROVISIONS

Josselin (by canal) All shops and
services

Guégon (2kms) Bakery

Lantillac (2.5kms) Bakery, grocery,
café

MAPS 28 & 29

ACCOMMODATION

Gîte d'Etape

1. M&Mme Turbaux (2.5kms) Arné, Crédin 02 97 38 97 49   15 places
Use of kitchen Horses Open all year

gites-arne.jimdo.com

REFRESHMENTS

2. Cadoret Crêperie des Forges (200m) north from Pont de Cadoret (lock 43) 02 97 75 38 49
creperiedesforges.com

3. Café de Cadoret

4. Les Forges Restaurant à l'Orée de la Forêt 02 97 75 31 81

Also a café at Les Forges

PROVISIONS

Pomeleuc Bar-épicerie (250m north of Lock 41 La Tertraie 1)

Les Forges grocery, *dépôt pain*

MAPS 30 & 31

ACCOMMODATION

Hotels

1. Hotel-restaurant de Rohan (100m) 15, Place de la Mairie, 56580 Rohan
12 rooms 02 97 38 56 82 or
06 26 52 94 07 www.hotel-le-rohan.fr

Chambres d'hôte

2. Villa Tranquillité (by canal) 6 rue de la Minoterie, 56580 Rohan.
Table d'hôte 02 97 38 58 68 or
06 76 10 12 49 www.villa-tranquillite.fr

3. Manoir du Quengo (300m)
Le Quengo, Rohan 3 manoir rooms plus 5 budget rooms (shared facilities) Horses Open all year
Swimming pool   02 97 25 50 68
manoirduquengo.com

4. Mme Le Pottier (500m) Rue Haute Ville, Rohan 02 97 51 50 39 4 rooms
Use of kitchen Horses Open all year.
http://haute-ville.jimdo.com

Camping

5. Camping Municipal du Val d'Oust (by canal) Route de Saint-Gouvry
56580 Rohan 02 97 51 57 58
45 places June to mid-Sept

REFRESHMENTS

Rohan (by canal)

6. Le Petit Tonneau - pizzeria (by canal) 1 rue Pont d'Oust
02 97 51 57 96

7. Hotel de Rohan – pizzeria (see above)

8. Restaurant L'Eau d'Oust 6 rue du Lac 02 97 38 91 86

9. Crêperie-Grill La Gavotte 4 Place de la Mairie 02 97 51 53 42

Crédin (3kms) - crêperie, café, bar

Bréhan (3.5kms) – restaurant, café, bars

PROVISIONS

Rohan (by canal)– all shops and services

Crédin (3kms) Bakery, grocery

Bréhan (3.5kms) Supermarket, bakery

MAPS 32 & 33

ACCOMMODATION

Chambres d'hôte

1. Fabienne Gicquel (1.5kms) La Cavalerie, 56920 St Gonnery.
2 rooms Use of kitchen Horses
Open all year Camping possible
02 97 38 42 56 or 06 33 69 27 81
www.gite-cavalerie-morbihan.com

2. Caux Breizh (800m) 10 rue du Stade, St-Samson, 56580 Rohan.
(groups up to 15) 02 97 38 99 12
06 62 78 11 85
www.cauxbreizh.jimdo.com

REFRESHMENTS

3. Saint-Gonnery (1.5kms) Crêperie La Rose des Vents Rue des Deux-Ponts 02 97 38 44 84 Closed 2nd half Sept.

4. Restaurant Chez Annick et Patrick (1.2kms) Rue des Deux-Ponts
02 97 38 40 90 Midday meals
Closed August

Gueltas café du Centre

PROVISIONS

Saint-Gonnery (1.2kms) Supermarket, *dépôt pain*, bakery

Gueltas (1.5kms) grocery, *dépôt pain*

MAPS 34 & 35

ACCOMMODATION

1. Hotel/Restaurant Le Théréza (by canal) Keroret 02 97 51 40 14

REFRESHMENTS

2. Keroret Hotel/Restaurant Le Théréza (by canal) 02 97 51 40 14

PROVISIONS

Saint-Gérand (600m) Grocery, bakery

MAPS 36 & 37

ACCOMMODATION

Hotels

1. Hotel-restaurant de l'Europe (1km) 12 rue François Mitterand 56300 Pontivy 20 rooms 02 97 25 11 14 www.hotellerieurope.com

2. Hotel-restaurant Martin (300m) 1 rue Leperdit 56300 Pontivy 02 97 25 02 04 23 rooms

3. Hotel Robic (1km) 4 rue Jean Jaurès, Pontivy 02 97 25 11 80 pontivy-hotel.com 29 rooms

4. Hotel du Château (100m) 41 rue général De Gaulle, Pontivy 28 rooms 02 97 25 34 88 hotel-duchateau@orange.fr www.hoteldepontivy.com

5. Hotel Le Rohan (800m) 90 rue Nationale, Pontivy 02 97 25 02 01 www.hotelpontivy.com 16 rooms

Chambres d'hôte

6. M&Mme Prouff (500m) 9 rue de Lourmel 02 97 25 07 52 laurent.prouff@wanadoo.fr 3 rooms Open all year

7. Mme Launay (300m) 18 rue de Gascogne 02 97 25 74 81 3 rooms Open all year moniquelaunay@wanadoo.fr

8. Mme Miloux (1.8kms) La Bretonnière, Bel Air, Neulliac 02 97 39 62 48 3 rooms miloux.bretonniere@wanadoo.fr Open all year

REFRESHMENTS

Pontivy – wide range of restaurants, crêperies, pizzerias, etc.

PROVISIONS

Pontivy – all shops and services

MAPS 38 & 39

ACCOMMODATION

Chambres d'hôte

1. M&Mme Le Boudec(by canal) Le Pont Guern 02 96 28 54 52 Open all year 3 rooms www.tycanal.com

2. M&Mme Raflé (3.5kms) Ferme de Lintever 02 97 38 03 95 4 rooms Use of kitchen www.fermedelintever.com

3. Mme Henrio (2.5kms) La Croix-Even, St Aignan 02 97 27 51 56 3 rooms

REFRESHMENTS

4. Le Corboulo (2km from Lock 114 Boloré or 1km from Lock 118 Quénécan) Restaurant Le Corboulo 02 97 27 50 14

Neulliac (1.5kms) Crêperie, café, bar

Cléguérec (6kms) Restaurants, bars

PROVISIONS

Neulliac (1.5) –grocery/bar, bank/cash point

Cléguérec (6kms) – range of shops, supermarket

MAPS 40 & 41

ACCOMMODATION

Hotels

1. Hotel/Restaurant Le Relais du Lac (2kms) Caurel 02 96 67 11 00 lerelaisdulac.jimdo.com

2. Auberge Grand Maison (2kms) Mûr-de-Bretagne 02 96 28 51 10 www.auberge-grand-maison.com

3. Hotel/Restaurant La Perrière (2kms) Mur-de-Bretagne 02 96 26 08 63 restaurant-hotel-murdebretagne.fr

Chambres d'hôte

4. M&Mme Menier (2kms) Favanic
Mûr-de-Bretagne 02 96 26 00 00
2 rooms Seasonal

5. M&Mme Partridge (2kms)
Mûr-de-Bretagne 02 96 26 05 79
www.pearblossomhouse.com
1 room Open all year

6. Ty Bara Kozh (1.4kms) 4 Place de
la Bascule, Le bourg, 22570
St-Gelven 02 96 36 90 66
www.bedandbreakfast-brittany.co.uk

Gîte d'Etape
7. Caurel (2kms) 02 96 67 11 00
16 places Open all year

Camping
8. Camping Le Guerledan & Les Pins
(by lake) Beau Rivage 02 96 26 08 24
/ 02 96 28 52 22 Open April to end
Sept 85 places

9. Camping Le Point de Vue (by lake)
Mûr-de-Bretagne Feb-Nov
02 96 26 01 90 133 places.
camping-lepointdevue@orange.fr

**10. Camping Merlin les Pieds dans
l'eau** (by lake) l'Anse de Sordan
02 97 27 52 36
www.restaurant-merlin.fr

11. Camping Rural de Quénécan (by
canal) 02 96 26 00 81 6 places

REFRESHMENTS
12. Le Corboulo (1km from Ecluse
118 Quénécan or 2km from Lock 114
Boloré) Restaurant Le Corboulo
02 97 27 50 14

13. Saint Aignan (1km) Crêperie du
Rohic 02 97 27 51 72 April - Sept

14. Saint Aignan (1km) Restaurant
Les Pêcheries 02 97 27 50 12

15. Beau Rivage (by lake)
L'Embarcadère (brasserie, crêperie,
plus dining cruises) 02 96 28 52 64
www.guerledan.com

16. Mûr-de-Bretagne (2kms) Le Mur a
Pizzas 02 56 07 99 98

Les Blés d'Or (crêperie, pizzeria, grill)
02 96 26 04 89

17. Caurel (2kms) Crêperie/Bar du
Vieux Moulin, Beau Rivage
02 96 28 54 72

18. Restaurant Merlin (by lake) Anse
de Sordan. 02 97 27 52 36
www.restaurant-merlin.fr

PROVISIONS
St-Aignan (1km) – *dépôt pain*,
groceries

Mûr-de-Bretagne (2kms) – all shops
and services

MAPS 42 & 43

ACCOMMODATION
Hotels
**1. Hotel-restaurant Les Jardins de
l'Abbaye** (100m) Abbaye de Bon
Repos 22570 Saint-Gelven. 5 rooms
02 96 24 95 77
lesjardinsdelabbaye@wanadoo.fr
abbaye.jardin.free.fr

Gîte d'Etape
2. Laniscat (4kms) 06 99 20 22 57
20 places Use of kitchen Horses
Open all year

3. Rando Accueil **La Gare de
Gouarec** (300m) 06 77 38 05 95
14 places Use of kitchen Open all
year

4. Mme Henneteau (500m) 7 rue du
Baron, 22570 Gouarec 02 96 24 91 99
or 06 86 04 45 04
christianhenneteau@yahoo.fr

Camping
5. Camping Tost Aven (400m by
canal) Le Bout du Pont, 22570
Gouarec (April - Sept) 02 96 27 87 86
06 03 35 19 65
campingdegouarec.fr

REFRESHMENTS
5. Bon Repos Crêperie-bar de Bon
Repos (500m) 02 96 24 86 56

6. Hotel-restaurant Les Jardins de
l'Abbaye (100m) 02 96 24 95 77

7. Cafe l'Abbaye (200m)
02 96 24 91 06 March – Sept

9. Gouarec Le Kost ar C'hoat
Pizzeria/ restaurant 02 96 24 99 97

10. Plélauff Restaurant Dour Pierre
(by canal) 1 Bout du Pont
02 96 24 90 74

11. Crêperie Au Bon Vieux Temps,
(by canal)16 Bout du Pont
02 96 24 82 95

PROVISIONS
Laniscat (4kms north of Bon Repos)
Bakery, groceries, bars,

Gouarec Bakeries, groceries,
supermarket, bank/cashpoint,

MAPS 44 & 45

ACCOMMODATION
Hotels
1. Hotel-restaurant Le Henri IV (4kms)
Route de Carhaix, 22110 Rostrenen
32 rooms 02 96 29 15 17
henri4-medicis@wanadoo.fr
www.henri4-medicis.fr

Chambres d'hôte
2. M&Mme Perrot (3kms) 40 rue du
Château Brulé 22110 Rostrenen
02 96 29 06 29 2 rooms Open all
year

3. Mme Burlot (3kms) 10 rue de la
Corderie 22110 Rostrenen
02 96 29 09 75 2 rooms Open all
year

4. Maison du Canal (by canal) Pont
Auffret, 22110 Rostrenen 4 rooms,
open all year 02 96 24 78 60
info@maisoncanal.com
www.maisoncanal.com

Gîte d'Etape
5. Ker Marc'h (3kms), 22110
Plouguernével 02 96 29 10 95
25 places Use of kitchen Camping
Open all year
www.plouguernevel.com/kermarch

Camping
6. Camping Fleur de Bretagne
(3.5kms) Kerandouaron
02 96 29 15 45 Open all year
www.fleurdebretagne.com

REFRESHMENTS
Rostrenen – restaurants, pizzerias,
crêperies

PROVISIONS
Rostrenen – supermarket, bakeries,
bank

Plélauff – bakery, bars

MAPS 46 & 47

ACCOMMODATION
Hotel
1. Hotel-restaurant La Cascade
5 Grande Rue 22110 Glomel
02 96 29 60 44 9 rooms

Chambres d'hôte
2. M&Mme Webb 5 place du Centre
22110 Glomel 02 96 29 88 44 Open
all year 4 rooms
brittanybedandbreakfast.net

Camping
3. Camping du Korong (2kms) Etang
du Corong 22110 Glomel
02 96 29 84 20 / 06 26 10 91 43
55 places Easter-Nov
www.lekorong.fr

REFRESHMENTS
4. La Pie, resto-routiers (near Lock
179 La Pie) 02 96 29 87 41

Glomel (2kms) - bar and café

PROVISIONS
Glomel (2kms)– bakery, grocery

Paule (2.5kms) – grocery, dépôt pain

MAPS 48 & 49

ACCOMMODATION
Hotels
1. Hotel Le Noz Vad (3.5kms) Carhaix
02 98 99 12 12 www.nozvad.bzh
44 rooms

2. Hotel-Bar d'Ahès (3.5kms) Carhaix
02 98 93 00 09 10 rooms
hotel-ahes.com

Chambres d'hôte
3. L'Asinerie du Pelem (by canal) Le
Pelem (between Locks 195 and 196)
02 98 99 44 21 www.lasdlp.com
Donkeys welcome and for hire

4. Manoir de Kerlédan (3kms)
M&Mme Dinwiddie 3 rooms (closed
in winter months) 02 98 99 44 63
www.kerledan.com

5. M&Mme Bournot (3.5kms) Carhaix
02 98 93 73 36 1 room
michelelebournot@hotmail.fr

Group accommodation

6. Le Centre d'Hébergement de Kerampuilh (3kms) Kerampuilh, Carhaix 02 98 99 37 97   90 places kerampuilh@aile29.org

7. Gîte d'étape communal Port-de-Carhaix 02 98 99 58 84   32 places Open all year

REFRESHMENTS

8. Port de Carhaix Auberge du Poher (250m on D769 south) 02 98 99 51 18 Closed Sunday evening and Monday auberge-du-poher.com

Carhaix (3kms north) has a wide range of restaurants.

PROVISIONS

Carhaix (3kms north) large town with many shops, supermarkets, banks, services of all kinds, and a railway station.

MAPS 50 & 51

ACCOMMODATION
Hotels
1.Hotel/Restaurant Les Bruyères (3.5kms) Spézet 02 98 93 80 19 9 rooms   grilladeslesbruyereshotel.com

Chambres d'hôte
2. Manoir de Toullaeron (5kms) Spézet 02 98 93 97 58   4 rooms Evening meal toullaeron@wanadoo.fr http://manoirdetoullaeron.webnode.fr

3. Les Chambres de l'Aulne (1km or 2.5kms from Pont Triffen) 11 rue de l'Aulne, Landelau   02 98 93 94 73 / 06 47 36 94 09 www.chambre-hote-landeleau.fr

Gîte for groups
Group accommodation
(individuals possible)

4. Presbital Kozh (1km, or 2.5kms from Pont Triffen) Landelau bourg. 15 places 02 98 93 93 08 07 82 78 24 37 gite-presbitalkozh-landeleau.bzh

Camping
5. Camping du Moulin Vert (800m) Pont Triffen 02 98 93 82 05 Open June, July, August Hire of rooms/caravans possible. a-pratulo.com

REFRESHMENTS

7. Pont Triffen Restaurant - Crêperie 02 98 93 92 99 Open every day in season, otherwise closed Wed.

St-Hernin (1.5kms)- café

Cléden-Poher (2.5kms)- café

Spézet (4kms) Restaurants, cafés

PROVISIONS

St-Hernin (1.5kms) Bakery, grocery, café

Cléden-Poher (2.5kms) Bakery, grocery, café

Landeleau (1km or 2.5kms from Pont Triffen) – bakery, grocery

Spézet (4kms)– bakery, grocery, bank/cash point

MAPS 52 & 53

ACCOMMODATION
Hotel
1. Hotel/Restaurant Le Relais de Cornouaille (800m) Châteauneuf (Logis de France) 29 rooms 02 98 81 75 36 relaisdecornouaille@wanadoo.fr http://lerelaisdecornouaille.com

Chambres d'hôte

2. Mme le Borgne (1km) Châteauneuf 02 98 73 21 93 yv.leborgne@laposte.net   2 rooms Open all year

3. M.Canévet (2.6kms from Pont du Stang) Kerdaffret, Spézet 02 98 93 80 60   2 rooms

4. Mme Patricia Louedec (1km) 17 rue Jean Dorval, 29520 Châteauneuf-du-Faou 02 98 99 78 41 http://aufildelaulne.com

5. Château Kervoazec (2kms) 29520 Saint-Goazec 03 89 83 90 67 - 02 98 26 86 91 chateau.kervoazec@orange.fr chateaukervoazec.com

6. The Old Bakery (500m) 19 Rue Paul Serusier, 29520 Châteauneuf-du-Faou tom.sarah@blueyonder.co.uk theoldbakery.org

Group accommodation
(individuals possible)

7. Maison Eclusière du Gwaker (by canal) 02 98 73 20 76 Open all year 27 places www.ulamir-aulne.com

8. Maison Eclusière Le Moustoir (by canal) 02 98 73 24 59 Open all year 15 places

Camping

9. Camping municipal du Goaker (300m) 02 98 26 82 20 30 places June to Sept www.ulamir-aulne.com

10. Camping de Penn ar Pont (200m) Châteauneuf 80 places June to Sept 02 98 81 81 25 pennarpont.com

Châteauneuf-du-Faou (400m) Bars, cafés and restaurants

11. Pizzeria Le Chaland, Châteauneuf (right by canal) 02 98 81 78 66

12. Aulne Loisirs, Châteauneuf (by canal) Snack bar 02 98 73 28 63 Seasonal

PROVISIONS

St-Goazec – bakery, grocery

Châteauneuf-du-Faou – shops, supermarkets, banks, all services

MAPS 54 & 55

ACCOMMODATION
Chambres d'hôte

1. Mme Floch (2kms) Lennon 02 98 72 71 28 2 rooms Open all year

Gîte for groups

2. Centre Ti Forn (2kms) St-Thois 02 98 73 20 76 46 places Open all year http://www.ulamir-aulne.fr

Camping

3. Camping de Stervinou (by canal) Le Stervinou, St-Thois 02 98 73 20 76 35 places April – Sept http://www.ulamir-aulne.fr

4. St Thois Café-restaurant de la Mairie (1.5kms) Open all year Mon - Fri (closed 2 weeks Aug & at Christmas) 02 98 73 83 29

PROVISIONS

Lennon (2kms) Bar (dépôt pain, groceries)

Pleyben (4.5kms) Shops, supermarket, banks, all services

St-Thois (1.5kms) Bakery, grocery

MAPS 56 & 57

ACCOMMODATION
Hotels

1. Hotel le Chrismas (200m) Logis de France Châteaulin 02 98 86 01 24 18 rooms le-chrismas@wanadoo.fr www.lechismas.com

2. Hotel de France (near canal) Châteaulin 6 rooms 02 98 86 11 26 htldefrance.e-monsite.com

Chambres d'hôte

3. The Old Forge House (600m) 56 Rue Graveran, Châteaulin 02 98 86 32 21 http://theoldforgehouse.webs.com

4. M Agouzoul (3kms) Leuriou, St-Coulitz 02 98 86 03 55 5 rooms

5. Mme Le Cann (500m) 8 rue Théodore Botrel, Châteaulin. 02 98 86 10 91 www.pennarpont.fr Open all year

Group accommodation (individuals possible)

6. Centre Herbergement du centre nautique (by canal) Pont Coblant 02 98 73 34 69 individuals and groups 56 places www.clubnautique-pleyben.fr

7.Centre de vacances du Vieux-Bourg (500m) Châteaulin 02 98 16 10 97 65 places Open all year Horses esat.chateaulin@lesgenetsdor.org

Camping

8. Camping Municipal (by canal) Pont Coblant 02 98 73 34 69 (mairie, Pleyben 02 98 26 71 05) 60 places June to Septr

9. Camping la Pointe Superbe (500m)
Route de St-Coulitz, Chateaulin
02 98 86 51 53
lapointecamping@aol.com
www.lapointesuperbecamping.com
60 places Mid-Mar - Mid-Oct

10. Camping Municipal de Rodaven
(near canal) 02 98 86 32 93 (Mairie)
campingderodaven.fr 100 places
June to September

REFRESHMENTS

Pont Coblant (by canal)

11. Auberge du Poisson Blanc (by
canal) Pont Coblant 02 98 73 34 76

auberge-poisson-blanc.fr

12. DELETE Crêperie Le Forestier (by
canal) 02 98 73 34 90 (seasonal)

13. Crêperie La Bohème (by canal)
02 98 73 37 97 (seasonal)

Pleyben (4.5kms) cafés, bars and
restaurants

Châteaulin (by canal) numerous
cafés, bars and restaurants

PROVISIONS

Pleyben (4.5kms) Shops,
supermarket, banks, all services

Châteaulin (by canal) Shops,
supermarkets, banks and all services.

MAP 58

ACCOMMODATION
Chambres d'hôte
1. Old Salt House (by canal) Port
Launay 02 98 86 28 85 06 06 46 21 09
Open all year 5 rooms
www.oldsalthouse.com

REFRESHMENTS

2. Bar-restaurant Guily Glas
02 98 86 29 06 (closed weekends and
3 weeks in August)

Port Launay (by canal) bar

PROVISIONS

Port Launay – bakery

Beyond the canal

ACCOMMODATION
Hotels
1. Hotel/Restaurant Le Saint-Patrick
Landévennec 02 98 27 70 83
7 rooms Open mid-March to mid-
Oct www.le-saint-patrick.fr

Chambres d'hôte

2. M&Mme Brindeau Ferme apicole
(Musée de l'abeille/Bee Museum)
Rosnoën 6 rooms 02 98 81 06 90
Open all year
www.ferme-apicole-de-terenez.com

3. Ferme Auberge du Seillou
Le Seillou Rosnoën M&Mme Le
Pape 02 98 81 92 21 5 rooms
www.fermeaubergeduseillou.com

4. Gîte Rando-Plume Ty Bihan
Kervézennec Rosnoën
M&Mme Le Guirriec 6 rooms
02 98 81 93 84 Open all year
www.gite-rando-bretagne.fr

5. Rando-Gîte Landévennec
02 98 27 72 65 (mairie) 26 places
landevennec.fr/gite-de-randonnee.htm

Camping

6. Camping du Seillou Le Seillou
Rosnoën 02 98 81 92 14 100 places
April to Sept

7. Camping municipal du Pal
Landévennec 02 98 27 72 65 (mairie)
May to Sept

REFRESHMENTS in Pont-de-Buis,
Rosnoën, Térénez, Landévennec and
Le Faou

PROVISIONS in Pont-de-Buis, Rosnoën
and Le Faou

Musée de la Batellerie, Redon

This museum, situated on the Quai Jean Bart by the marina in the old port, is essential viewing for canal enthusiasts. An introductory and atmospheric video about life on the canal has an English version, and there is then the opportunity to negotiate a boat through a lock on a scale-model and browse many documents, photos and implements from the social and economic history of the canal.

Open every day from mid-June to mid-September, otherwise Sat, Sun & Mon afternoons. Closed mid November to early April. www.redon.fr (tourisme/musee de la batellerie)

Swing-bridge in Redon at the crossing of the Vilaine

Musée de la Batellerie

Locks on the Nantes-Brest Canal

Lock no.		kms	Lock no.		kms
1	St-Félix	0	55	Coët-Prat	185.8
2	Quiheix	21.7	56	Kermelin	186.8
3	La Tindière	26.2	57	La Sablière	187.2
4	La Rabinière	28.9	58	Keriffé	187.5
5	La Haie Pacoret	30.0	59	Boju	187.8
6	Cramezeul	31.0	60	Le Parc-Cob	188.0
7	Pas d'Héric	32.3	61	Le Goiffre	188.1
8	La Remaudais	40.6	62	Goirbal	188.5
9	Gué de l'Atelier	43.7	63	Guernogas	188.8
10	Le Terrier	45.4	64	Branguily	189.0
11	Blain - La Prée	48.7	65	La Naue-Blanche	189.2
12	Paudais	51.5	66	Le Pont-Terre	189.3
13	Bougard	56.2	67	La Forêt	189.5
14	Barelle	59.4	68	Menn-Merle	198.7
15	La Touche	61.8	69	Toulhouët	189.9
16	Melneuf	65.9	70	La Ville Perro	190.1
17	Les Bellions	88.7	71	Le Gouvly	190.2
17bis	Redon-Isac	94.9	72	Pont	190.4
18	Redon-Oust	95.0	73	Kervézo	190.6
19	La Maclais Painfaut	105.3	74	Le Douaren	190.8
20	Limur	109.8	75	Le Grand-Pré	190.9
21	Le Gueslin	116.6	76	Hilvern	191.1
22	Rieux	120.4	77	La Pépinière	191.2
23	Beaumont	125.5	78	Bel-Air	191.4
24	Foveno	129.6	79	Kéroret	196.3
25	Malestroit	132.6	80	Er Houët	196.4
26	La Née 1	134.4	81	Kerivy	196.5
27	La Née 2	135.4	82	Parc-er-Lann	196.7
28	Ville-aux-Fruglins	139.7	83	Kerihoué	196.8
29	Montertelot	143.6	84	Parc-Lann-Bihan	196.9
30	Blond	146.2	85	Lann-Vras	197.1
31	Guillac	149.0	86	Parc-Buisson	197.2
32	Carmenais	152.1	87	Le Couédic	197.3
33	Clan	154.1	88	Joli-Cœur	199.7
34	St-Jouan	155.6	89	Parc-Lann-Hir	199.8
35	Josselin	157.3	90	Parc-Lann-Ergo	199.9
36	Beaufort	158.4	91	Parc-Bihan	200.0
37	Caradec	159.8	92	Kerponer	200.1
38	Rouvray	161.4	93	Restériard	200.3
39	Bocneuf	163.1	94	Tri-Parc-Lann-Favilet	200.4
40	Pomeleuc	165.6	95	Parc-Bras	200.6
41	La Tertraie 1	165.9	96	Le Roz	200.7
42	La Tertraie 2	167.2	97	Guerlaunay	200.8
43	Cadoret	169.7	98	Bohumet	201.1
44	Le Lié	170.9	99	Kervégan	201.3
45	Griffet	172.4	100	Tren-deur-Roz	202.0
46	La Grenouillère	173.3	101	Kerveno	202.3
47	Trévérend	174.2	102	Parc-Lann-Houarem	202.8
48	Penhouët	175.4	103	La Haie	203.5
49	L'Île	176.4	104	La Villeneuve	204.0
50	Timadeuc	178.4	105	Kerdudaval	204.5
51	Quengo	180.5	106	Kervert	205.1
52	Rohan	181.4	107	Le Ponteau	205.5
53	St-Samson	183.6	108	La Cascade	207.1
54	Le Guer	184.8	109	Guernal	209.4

Index

Index